Penguin Books
AFTER THE PARTY

In 1969 Barry Cohen was elected to the House of Representatives Seat of Robertson on the Central Coast of New South Wales, capturing a seat held by the Liberals for the previous 20 years. He has been re-elected at eight successive elections.

In the first two Hawke Ministries he held the position of Minister for Home Affairs and Environment which was later named Arts, Heritage and Environment. He has also been the Minister responsible for the Bicentennial and the Minister Assisting the Prime Minister for the Bicentennial throughout that period.

He was born in Griffith in 1935 and is married with three sons.

AFTER THE PARTY
MORE POLITICAL ANECDOTES

Barry Cohen
Illustrations by Bruce Petty

Penguin Books

Penguin Books Australia Ltd
487 Maroondah Highway, PO Box 257
Ringwood, Victoria, 3134, Australia
Penguin Books Ltd
Harmondsworth, Middlesex, England
Viking Penguin Inc.
40 West 23rd Street, New York, NY 10010, USA
Penguin Books Canada Limited
2801 John Street, Markham, Ontario, Canada, L3R 1B4
Penguin Books (N.Z.) Ltd
182-190 Wairau Road, Auckland 10, New Zealand

First published by Penguin Books Australia, 1988

Copyright © Barry Cohen, 1988

All Rights Reserved. Without limiting the rights under copyright
reserved above, no part of this publication may be reproduced,
stored in or introduced into a retrieval system, or transmitted,
in any form or by any means (electronic, mechanical, photocopying,
recording or otherwise), without the prior written permission
of both the copyright owner and the above publisher of this
book.

Typeset in 10½ point Caledonia Roman by Leader Composition Pty Ltd
Made and printed in Australia by Australian Print Group, Maryborough, Victoria

CIP

Cohen, Barry, 1935- .
After the party, more political anecdotes.

Includes index.
ISBN 0 14 011738 5.

1. Politicalsatire, Australian. 2. Australia –
Politics and government – 1965- – Anecdotes.
III. Title.

994.06

To Gough, without whom *The Life of the Party* and *After the Party* would have been incomplete

CONTENTS

Acknowledgements	ix
Preface	xi
Call Me Minister	1
Dear Voter	27
Life with Gough	43
The Meeja	55
Around the House	63
Around the World	71
Our Man In . . .	85
The Party at Play	93
The First Lady	115
In the Shop	139
Where the Buck Stops	147
In the Wild	161
Index of Names	181

ACKNOWLEDGEMENTS

Once again there are many people to thank. Kathy Lette and my wife, Rae, have been an enormous source of encouragement as have been my three sons, Stuart, Martin and Adam. There could have been no greater boost to my confidence than to come across the usually reserved Adam crying with laughter as he read the draft of this book. To John and Barbara Vyden who kept up the encouragement from Los Angeles, and my marvellous literary agent Jill Hickson a special thanks. Once again Jacquie Spring and Rosanne Ransley performed miracles with their word processors and put up with my never-ending alterations and corrections.

As in *Life of the Party*, a small number of quotes from *Hansard*, political speeches by prominent politicians and press conferences came from earlier publications. These are all public documents, but I am grateful that someone else had done the tedious work of collecting them.

It was suggested to me that one or two of the stories in *Life of the Party* were apocryphal. What I can say is this. Seventy-five percent of the stories happened to me, so I can assure readers that's exactly how they occurred. The others have been recounted to me by friends and colleagues and I have no reason to doubt their veracity. To Fred Daly, Eric Walsh, Alan Ramsay, John Button, Tony Sansom, Graham Freudenberg, John Tingle, Bob Brown, Lionel Bowen,

David Connolly, John Wheeldon, Jim McClelland, Dick Klugman, Dean Wells, John Mildren, John Dawkins, James Mollison, Colin Hollis, Paul Eddington and Peter Doyle, my heartfelt thanks. Sergio Sergi, my former Senior Private Secretary and now interim director of the National Maritime Museum, deserves a very special mention. I am indebted to him for the many hilariously funny episodes from his diplomatic career and also for reminding me of events that occurred when we were working together.

One comment made by a number of people was that very few of my stories were about Liberal or National Party Members. It's a fair comment. My only explanation is that I obviously spend more time with my Labor colleagues than I do with our opponents. I approached a number of Coalition Members to see what I could get, but with one or two exceptions I was unsuccessful. Now, I think the Liberals are a scream and the Nationals hilarious but I think it will have to be done by my opposite number in the Coalition. Over to you fellas.

PREFACE

Apart from being elected to Parliament in 1969 and to the Ministry in 1983, I don't think anything has given me such a thrill as the publication of my first book, *The Life of the Party*. The writing, publishing, marketing and promotion of the book were all totally new experiences for me and ones that were immensely rewarding. When I realised how much fun I was having, I knew I had the writer's bug. *The Life of the Party* hadn't hit the bookshops before I was planning my next effort. Kathy Lette had told me that my biggest thrill would come when I saw my first book in a shop. However, when that happened, I started worrying about why they hadn't all sold. When I came back next week, I started worrying about why the shop hadn't reordered, or whether Penguin was out of stock. I used to look at all the thousands of books in the shop and think, 'How will anyone notice my little book?' or 'Why isn't it out at the front in a massed display?' When my Uncle Joe rang to tell me that he had been to four shops to buy a book and they had all sold out, I nearly had my second heart attack. Poor John Curtain and Mark Sheehan of Penguin – I nearly drove the poor fellows mad! I don't know what they said behind my back, but they were very patient with me.

I have had a number of complimentary letters about my first book, but nothing to match the following endorsement. It stands alone without comment.

Dear Mr Cohen,

My dear wife, blissfully innocent of all things political, recently gave me a copy of your book, *The Life of the Party*, as a Father's Day present. As the wife of an arch conservative, she was somewhat crestfallen when I informed her that the author of the book was a Labor politician.

As the book purported to be of a humorous nature, I was able to salve her hurt feelings with the observation that as it was written by a Bolshie it would have to be a joke.

However, you will no doubt be pleased to learn that the raucous laughter emanating from my study has satisfied her that she made a wise choice in the selection of my present.

As a former Administrative Manager of a light aircraft charter company in Papua New Guinea, I am particularly aware that flying in such circumstances is 10% boredom and 90% stark terror. Hence I was able to identify with the obvious discomfort referred to in your chapter 'Fear of Flying'. The fact that the said discomfort was suffered by a socialist added to my enjoyment.

Although I cannot, in my wildest nightmares, contemplate ever voting for your thieving socialist party, I assure you that I will not hesitate to purchase a sequel to your book, should you care to publish one.

In all likelihood your place in history will be secured in the company of Henry Lawson and Banjo Paterson as making a valuable contribution to Australian literature, rather than for whatever it is you do with yourself in Canberra.

Yours faithfully.
ROBERT STAINES

The critics were kind, too. Suddenly, instead of being torn to pieces by Liberals, Democrats, Nationals, journalists of all sectors of the media and complaining constituents, I found everyone was very friendly. Invited to speak all over the country and tell some of the stories from the book, all I found was laughing, smiling, friendly people. No one disagreed. No one abused me. No one attacked me. 'This is better than politics,' I thought, 'and I get paid as well.'

In all the reviews there was only criticism: I had not provided any insight into the 'behind-the-scenes' drama that led to my dumping by the numbers men of the machine. There was a simple explanation for that. It hadn't happened when the book went to the publishers. However, even if it had, I wanted people to have a good laugh. People already know that politics can be nasty. They get that every time they pick up the papers, turn on the TV, or listen to the radio. If they ever go to Parliament, or worse, join a political party, they'll really know how nasty politics can become. For a change, I wanted people to see the funny, even ridiculous side of politics. To understand that beneath all that brawling, there was a human side to politics. I hope people enjoy reading *After the Party* as much as I enjoyed writing it.

CALL ME MINISTER

CONFESSIONS OF A FEATHER DUSTER

(From the *Bulletin* Christmas Issue, December 1987)

It is now about five months since I ceased to be the Minister for Arts, Heritage and Environment. Friends approach me tremulously enquiring about my health and state of mind. 'Hello, how are you .. ?' 'Well, frankly I've never felt better!' 'Yes, but . . . but how are you REALLY?' 'Look, I REALLY feel terrific, I've never enjoyed myself so much in my life,' I emphasise, knowing that I'm not being believed. 'Stout fella, that's the spirit! Don't let the bastards grind you down. You've taken it wonderfully!' they cry, as they grasp me to their bosom and depart with moistened eyes. Others tell me how they had wanted to ring or write, but 'just didn't know what to say'.

It's no good, I can't go on living a lie. The time has come to confess all. I am desperately miserable . . . distraught . . . beside myself with grief at no longer being a Federal Minister. The humiliation and disgrace are there for all to see. It's called the 'feather duster' syndrome. Reduced to penury by having to live on the salary of a humble backbencher, I have had to start buying Australian suits again. With frayed cuffs, a slightly pinched look and with eyes averted, I shuffle past my friends and hear them mutter, 'Shame . . . once great man . . . let himself go . . .'

I have had to learn to drive again – a harrowing experience, and, with only three personal staff, the mysteries of the modern telephone system have had to be relearned. It is extraordinary the changes that have taken place in only five years!

The most demeaning part of all, however, is being called 'Barry' again. Unlike some nations, where ministerial titles are for life, Australia insists on remaining damnably egalitarian. No one calls me 'Minister' any more. But these are only the minutiae. The real loss is in the lifestyle. God, how I miss it!

Once life used to begin at 5 am on Monday morning. Now I am forced to sleep until 7.30 am, before enjoying breakfast in bed with the papers. No longer do I dress in the dark, then make a quick dash to Kingsford-Smith, before flying to Canberra for Cabinet at 9 am.

Few have experienced the thrill of waiting expectantly for the call to Cabinet for all of Monday . . . and Tuesday . . . and Wednesday . . . and then it comes and you dash up the stairs two at a time and arrive panting in the Cabinet room to be greeted by the dulcet tones of HIMSELF: 'Where the f...ing hell have you been? We've all been waiting for ages!' 'I came as soon as I was called,' you explain, only to be told lovingly, 'Well, get on with it, we haven't got all day!' 'No, only three days,' you mutter *sotto voce*. 'What was that?' he snarls back, as the eyes roll round like poker machine tumblers. Who would want to miss all that?

It's the friendly atmosphere of Cabinet that I miss most. With the welcoming introduction over, the friendly chat begins. 'More money for Arts, Barry? No worries!' are Peter Walsh's introductory remarks. 'Five million? Are you sure that's enough?' My main problem whenever arts submissions were before Cabinet was in keeping the debate to strictly monetary matters. Walsh and Duffy would digress into long philosophical discussions on the merits of Abstractionist versus Realist art. No sooner would they stop their incessant point scoring when Gordon Scholes and Stewart West would become involved in a furious debate over the direction of Australian dance. Time wasting it may have been, but boring . . . never! Those riveting deliberations were meat and drink to those of us starved of intellectual stimulation in the outside world.

The highlights of any Cabinet debates were always those that involved the lovely and talented Senator Evans. Humble and unassuming, it was always fun to be involved in a joint submission with Gareth. Prior to the matter coming to Cabinet, it was usually necessary to have a preliminary chat or ten with him to sort out any minor differences, like whether we should mine Kakadu National Park from top to bottom, or flood it with contaminated water from the Ranger retention ponds. These were fun meetings with Gareth, who was always sweetness and light and prepared to see everyone else's point of view.

One of these 'chats' with Clyde Holding and me commenced with the silent senator announcing to us that his wife had threatened to divorce him if he were successful in this particular submission. 'She's an intelligent woman, however, and I'm confident that if I take her through it step by step, she'll see the logic of my position.' 'Wonderful,' I said, 'now all you need is enough time to sit down with all the other women in Australia who care about the environment, and we'll have no problem.' I'll really miss my little 'chats' with Gareth.

Cabinet is only the tip of the iceberg. God, how I miss the Fourth Estate. Those early morning wake-up calls. 'Is that you, Barry, it's Michael here ... from "AM". I'm sorry to disturb you ...' (And you knew how genuinely sorry they were from the tone of their voice.) 'What time is it, Michael ... 5.30 am ... oh, how nice to hear from you so early. What is it you want to know?'

The media ring first thing in the morning for the same reason that police make early morning arrests. They get the suspect while he is still half asleep. Those who don't ring at 5.30 am wait until 7 pm on Sunday night. There you are, curled up in front of the telly with the spaghetti bolognaise and your wife and three sons, enjoying watching Norths thrash Parramatta (sic), and it rings. 'Michelle here, is that you Barry? I'm sorry to disturb you (they can't help themselves) ... about this Cabinet submission tomorrow.' 'Michelle, you know I can't talk about that,' I say, spitting spaghetti all over my wife's clean floor. 'Yes, I know you can't, but does your submission say .., I just want to clarify Clyde's ... will you be telling the PM?' I'll miss you too, Michelle.

Back in the electorate there will be things I miss too. I once worked out that in twenty-five years as a member of the Labor Party, MP, and Minister, I had probably attended over 2,000 Labor Party branch meetings. They were real fun. 'Unity of Labor is the Hope of the World' is our slogan and it was only after some years of attending State conferences that I realised what it meant – 'If Labor is united, there is hope for the rest of the world.' My local Federal Electorate Council, as a gesture of friendship after my eighteen years of service as their member, passed a no-confidence motion in me for missing the previous few meetings. It made me feel all warm inside. Still, when the Right's away, the Left will play.

I really hate the life I'm leading now, working only fifty hours a week, playing golf twice a week, reading novels and having dinner with friends, spending six nights a week at home with my family. I hate it, but in time I'll get used to it. In the meantime, I'll try hard not to miss being called 'Minister'.

The only thing I don't miss is having Ros Kelly hovering around my office with a tape measure, eyeing the drapes, every time a rumour circulated that my health was not the best.

TIME'S UP!

Becoming a 'feather duster' and the speed with which it happened should have come as no great shock to me after the experience of my good friend John Wheeldon, Senator for Western Australia from 1964-81, and Minister for Social Security when the Whitlam Government was sacked.

A few days after the event, John had only just returned to his office in Perth and was sitting there quietly writing when two workmen appeared.

'Yes?' enquired the former Minister.

'Gotta get the clock,' said the burliest of the two.
'What clock?'
'That clock,' he replied, pointing to the electric clock affixed to the wall behind John.
'Why?'
'Because it's ministerial issue and you ain't a minister no more!'

THE FRIENDLY WAY

Senators and MPs from Western Australia are a special breed. They have to be to survive the tortuous journey to and from Perth every week. So it is not surprising that when they settle down on the long flight over the continent, equal in distance to the flight from London to Moscow, they may relax with a drink or three to help them while away the time.

So it was that during the reign of 'John the Jolly' in the year of our Lord 1969, Senator Malcolm Scott, Minister for Customs and Excise, set forth on the long journey westward, comforted in the knowledge that he would have some assistance in getting to sleep.

Unfortunately for the Minister, he was accompanied by two fellow sandgropers who were colleagues of his in the Liberal Party, Senator Peter Sim (1964-1981) and Fred Chaney Snr, the Member for Perth (1955-1969) and a former Minister for the Navy. Aware that the journey could be tedious, they decided that the good Minister should have a voyage he would long remember. They approached the air hostess.

Flashing their gold passes, they informed her that they were Detective Inspector Sim and Sergeant Chaney and that they were taking a prisoner back to Perth to stand trial.

'Don't be alarmed!' said 'Inspector Sim'. 'He's not dangerous, that's why he's not handcuffed.' The young lady, whose eyes had widened with alarm when for a moment she had imagined a mad axe killer loose on the plane, relaxed at the assurances of the 'police'.

'He's quite alright,' said 'Sergeant Chaney'. 'The only problem is that he has these delusions that he's a Senator and the Federal Minister for Customs and Excise, but he only gets dangerous if he has anything to drink. See that he doesn't have any!'

The plane was not far out of Canberra when drinks were being served. Senator Scott settled down in anticipation. It wasn't long before he noticed that everyone else had drinks but him.

'Excuse me, young lady, but would you mind getting me a whisky?' asked the Minister politely.

'I'm sorry, but I can't.'

'What do you mean, you can't?'

'I just can't!'

'Why not?' asked the Senator.

'Because I'm not allowed to.'

'You're what?'

'I'm not allowed to!'

'But everyone else is getting a drink,' he snorted.

'Yes, they are, but you're not getting any,' she told him firmly.

'Why the hell not?' By now he was shouting.

'Because you become dangerous when you drink!'

'I WHAT??' he screamed. 'DO YOU KNOW WHO I AM?'

'Yes,' she smiled sweetly. 'You're the Federal Minister for Customs and Excise, but you're still not getting anything to drink!'

Nigel Bowen (Liberal) — September 1971
Minister for Foreign Affairs
The so-called Pentagon Papers are, of course, a selective set of papers from the records of the Pentagon.

THE ONLY ONE IN STEP

Two of the finest intellects that ever graced the red leather benches of the Australian Senate were Jim McClelland and John Wheeldon. It is to the eternal shame of the Labor Party that neither was in the first Whitlam ministry. Factional alignments, seniority and plain jealousy forced them to wait in the wings until the Caucus woke up to the fact that some of the initial choices weren't all that bright. Their addition to the Ministry lifted the average IQ about twenty percentage points.

Ideological labels as distinct from factional alignments are fairly meaningless in the Australian political context, but I'm sure neither would argue that during their parliamentary careers John was identified closely with the Left and Jim with the Right. At no stage did their labels interfere with their close friendship.

Walking 'home' to the Hotel Canberra from Parliament House, the two Ministers often indulged in long philosophical discussions about the meaning of life in general and Government intervention in the marketplace in particular. As they wended their way down King's Terrace to their destination, the flow of conversation seemed to be interrupted constantly by streams of public servants crisscrossing their path.

'Blast these public servants,' snarled Labor's Minister for Social Security. 'No matter where you move, the bastards are under your feet.'

'But John,' purred 'Diamond Jim', Labor's Minister for Labour and Immigration, 'I thought you wanted everyone to be a public servant?' Jim had expected his remark to be a telling point in their philosophical argument but he had never anticipated that it would have quite the effect on the Left's ideological guru that it did.

The good Senator stopped dead in his tracks and stiffened as if struck by a bolt of lightning. The look on his face of shock, horror and blinding revelation combined told Jim that he had hit the mark.

'Good God!' gasped the non-believer, 'I never thought of it like that!'

NO, MINISTER!

With Don McMichael being appointed to head up the National Museum of Australia, I was keen that his deputy, Pat Galvin, should get the appointment as Permanent Head of the Department of Home Affairs and Environment. The bureaucracy was equally determined that he should not. One could hear them muttering to themselves, 'Next thing, the politicians will want to run the country!'

After a long bureaucratic process that took months, I was confronted by three senior mandarins who had produced a short list of five that included Pat, but did not have him at the top of the list. I dug my heels in and was determined that whatever blandishments were offered, I would stick to my guns. A range of options was suggested but I rejected them all.

'Would you perhaps consider one of the existing Permanent Heads?' the senior mandarin enquired. 'Yes, of course,' I replied.

In unison they asked, 'Which one?'

'Any of you three gentlemen would be excellent,' I answered, knowing how they would crawl over broken glass to take on Home Affairs and Environment. Their faces fell a foot.

'Look, gentlemen,' I asked, 'what exactly have you got against Galvin? He's bright, he's hard working, he's loyal, he knows the portfolio backwards and we work well together. He'd make an excellent Permanent Head!'

There was a long pause and lots of clearing of throats and harrumphing until finally the senior mandarin spoke.

'Well, Minister,' (he was sounding more like Sir Humphrey every moment), 'let me put it this way. If Galvin were to get the job it would not be seen as an inspired appointment.' I had difficulty keeping a straight face. 'What exactly do you mean?' I enquired innocently, knowing exactly what he meant. Galvin had not been to the right school, didn't belong to the right clubs, was a Catholic with a father who had been the Labor MP for Kingston in South Australia for fifteen years. He also had a talented wife who was known for speaking her mind and sporting a punk hairdo.

There was another long, uncomfortable pause and he finally confirmed what I had been thinking. 'Well, he would be seen to lack the stature for the position.'

(Pat Galvin became Permanent Head of the Department until shortly after my period as Minister ended. He retired to Brisbane when his wife, Dr Lenore Manderson, was appointed to the Chair of Anthropology at Griffith University.

He was widely regarded as one of the best appointments made by the present Government and has since been appointed to one of the most prestigious part-time positions in Government – Chairman of the Australian Heritage Commission.)

THE WINDS OF CHANGE

My library is my prized possession. Among my 3,000 odd books, I have specialised sections on Australian politics and history, the Middle East, South Africa, the environment and diets. The last is the largest. I have every diet book ever printed, from Scarsdale to Pritikin, from the Beverley Hills Diet to the Israeli Army diet, which I was assured, when in Israel, appeared to be known to everyone but the Israeli Army.

Pride of place, however, belongs to the *F-Plan Diet*, given to me by my Research Assistant, Tony Sansom, who like myself, has devoted much of his life to attempting to shed surplus kilos.

'Try this!' he suggested prior to my departure in July 85 for an official visit to Norfolk Island, handing me a copy of the book.

'What's it like?' I asked.

'Excellent, you just eat lots of fibre, particularly beans,' he replied.

Well, as I liked baked beans, I thought, 'Why not?' I set off for the airport and the VIP plane that was to take our delegation to Norfolk, armed with a dozen tins of Heinz's best. On board, our steward had gone to a great deal of trouble to prepare attractive and varied meals for breakfast and lunch. He was not particularly impressed when I handed him the tins of baked beans with the instructions. 'This is all I'll be eating, thank you, steward.'

For two days I ate nothing but baked beans – breakfast, lunch and dinner. A little monotonous as I watched my wife Rae and my Senior Private Secretary Sergio Sergi devour all the delicacies prepared by the descendants of the Bounty mutineers.

Baked beans are fine, in fact they are an excellent fare, ideal for a quick Saturday lunch. But they are NOT recommended as a staple diet unless you are at home among close members of the family. They are certainly not the ideal food for a Federal Minister undertaking a goodwill tour of a sparsely populated place like Norfolk Island.

It did not take long for the F-Plan to work. Rae and Sergio started to make excuses to be in everyone else's company but mine. She is normally an uncomplaining soul, but the dear girl got decidedly irritable when I kept her awake all night snoring and did more terrible things to her during the day – thanks to the beans.

I almost got used to her assailing me with a pillow for snoring during the evenings, but it was a little difficult for the long-suffering lady to belt me one during the day, surrounded as I was by senior public servants from both the Federal and Territory governments.

Everything came to a climax when the Norfolk Island Administrator put on an excellent cocktail party at his magnificent 150-year-old convict-built brick home at Kingston. Here I met the elected members of the Norfolk Island Legislative Assembly and the distinguished members of the 2,000-odd island community.

Guests gathered on the large classic colonial verandah, sipping pink gins and champagne and nibbling canapés. It was, I imagine, a scene reminiscent of the Raj, as the visiting Governor wandered around chatting with the native princes. It may have looked like a scene of imperial splendour and grace. It may well have sounded like one. It did not, I can assure you, smell like one.

As I wandered from group to group, the F-Plan had its effect. Guests parted like the Red Sea. Within half an hour, I had cleared the decks. They still talk about my visit to Norfolk Island with bated breath.

OUT OF THE FRYING PAN

The Office of the Supervising Scientist (OSS), was set up in 1978 by Malcolm Fraser as part of the package to get uranium mining started in the Kakadu region, some 200 kilometres from Darwin.

It was a strange quirk of fate that put one of the richest uranium deposits in the world smack-bang in the middle of one of the earth's richest and most diverse ecosystems. Superb wetlands, a rich flora and fauna, including 250 different species of birds, alongside a number of tribal Aboriginal communities, ensured that the value system of the miners and the conservationists would clash.

The job of the OSS was to monitor the impact of uranium on the surrounding environment. It was a very important task that required every one of the seventy-odd scientists and back-up staff provided. Malcolm promised Bob Fry, a prominent nuclear physicist, that if he accepted the position of Supervising Scientist, nothing would be spared to do the job properly. Bob accepted, but the Government immediately started back-tracking on its commitment.

I had only been the Minister for the Environment a few months when I undertook a round Australia trip, visiting the major national parks for which I was responsible. After visiting the Great Barrier Reef, I flew to Kakadu where Bob and his staff were waiting to show me around.

In the short period I had known Bob, I was not unfamiliar with his complaint that his staff in Kakadu were being seriously disadvantaged by insufficient housing, inadequate laboratories, and almost non-existent recreational facilities.

Having inspected the staff housing and been made very aware by Bob of the need for more if he were to retain top people in the appallingly hot, humid climate of the Top End, I was given a similar tour of the laboratories and staff amenities. Not being of a scientific bent, I simply walked around, trying to look intelligent, as I had explained to me the intricacies of a vast mass of impressive-looking equipment. I had to accept Bob's word that it was not up to scratch.

Finally we arrived at what was laughingly described as the staff's recreational quarters. A large slab of concrete, covered with canvas and equipped with an old fridge, an even older table tennis table, and some 'Early Revesby' lounge chairs.

'Sit down and I'll make you a cup of tea,' said Bob, as he picked up a cup and saucer that looked as if they should have been condemned years ago.

'Love one,' said I, as I collapsed on the sofa, wondering what this place must be like in the Wet. Collapsed is the operative word. I went straight through the lounge and bounced off the concrete floor!

There was a stunned silence from the OSS staff, broken

only by the wind escaping from my lungs. As I was finally extricated from this unministerial position, I turned to Bob, 'I think you've made your point. No need to go to all that trouble again!'

ALL THE WORLD'S A STAGE

'Would you like to present the National Theatre awards next year?' enquired my Senior Private Secretary, Peter Conway.

'Certainly!' I replied, honoured that I was to be the number one man at such a prestigious event. 'Where and when are they on?' I asked.

'Ballarat on 10 February next year. They're going to be televised,' Peter added.

'Wonderful! Don't forget to let John Mildren know that I've accepted. (John, the member for Ballarat, was both a colleague and close friend, who had won and held this very difficult rural seat from the Liberals.) He'll be delighted.' And so was I, as I contemplated the nation tuning in to yours truly as I made a stunning speech and had them alternatively rolling in the aisles or dabbing away the tears. 'Clive James and Graham Kennedy eat your heart out!' I thought as I immediately started making mental notes for my 'Address to the Nation'.

John was delighted, and as the event drew closer he arranged for my visit to be extended to see other parts of his electorate.

'You must be very thrilled to be having such a prestigious event in Ballarat,' I commented a couple of times to John, who was surprisingly quiet, for one who is not known for his long periods of silence.

Considerable preparation was made for our visit to Ballarat as speeches, briefings, and itinerary were checked carefully by staff, but the major effort was reserved for the

National Theatre awards.

The big night arrived and our entourage headed for the venue. I was more than a little surprised when I arrived at the recreated historic mining village of Sovereign Hill, but satisfied my curiosity that this was a novel place to hold such a gala function.

Our host for the evening greeted me at the front of the 'New York Bakery'.

'Minister!' he cried excitedly, 'It's so good of you to come all the way down here to the National Theatre of Ballarat to present the awards to our local amateurs!'

Out of the corner of my eye I glimpsed John Mildren suddenly finding an excuse to talk to the TV crew, who were setting up a video camera to record for posterity a 30-second clip for the local Ballarat TV station.

A NEAR MS

Rae and I, together with my Senior Private Secretary, Sergio Sergi, and his wife, Leigh, were invited to a dinner at the Italian Ambassador's residence in Canberra. Like many women who are married to a volatile and complex character, Leigh is inclined to stay in the background as Sergio entertains the crowd. Leigh is nevertheless a highly intelligent and attractive personality, but considerably less controversial than her explosive spouse.

Among the other guests were John Brown, the Minister for Sport and Tourism, and his wife, Jan.

After the usual pre-dinner drinks, guests were ushered into the spacious dining-room, where they began searching for their name cards beside the place settings.

Suddenly there was a kerfuffle at one end of the room, and guests heard the icy voice of the Sport and Tourism Minister's wife as her eyes alighted on her card. 'I AM NOT MRS JOHN BROWN!' she cried, loud enough to ensure that everyone in the room heard. 'I AM MS JAN MURRAY!' Guests froze, then shuffled awkwardly around during the interminable silence.

Eventually, the softly spoken Leigh broke the silence: 'Jan, if you were Ms Jan Murray, you wouldn't have been invited.'

THE BIG, THE BAD AND THE BEAUTIFUL

The increasing popularity of Jack Newton's annual Pro-Am celebrity golf tournament at Noosa in December 1986 attracted a star-studded field of Australia's top professional golfers and celebrities, including Greg Chappell, Dennis Lillee, Ricky May, 'Aussie Joe' Bugner, the Prime Minister and even Tourist Minister John Brown and myself.

With the temperature at 35 degrees Celsius and 90 per cent humidity, I staggered around the course in a respectable 85, in the delightful company of golf star Ian Baker-Finch, before returning to my hotel for a long bath and cool drink in preparation for dining with the Browns later that evening.

Still exhausted and clad only in a bath-robe, I was relaxing in front of the television waiting for them when the phone rang. It was the desk clerk.

'Mr Cohen?'
'Yes.'
'Mr and Mrs Bugner are here to see you.'
'Who?'
'Mr and Mrs Bugner.'
'I don't know any Mr and Mrs Bugner.'
'Joe and Marlene Bugner.'
'I don't know them either.'
'Well, they say they're coming up for a drink.'

I had recalled seeing 'Aussie Joe' at the golf that day. 'Built like a brick shithouse' was the phrase that came immediately to mind. I looked down at the paunchy midriff and tried to recall my last boxing triumph, when I had won CII division at Sydney Grammar School in 1945. I remembered that Joe had twice gone the distance with Mohammed Ali.

'Mr Cohen?' said the young man on the other end of the phone, by now starting to sound a little nervous himself. 'What shall I tell them?'

'Tell them to come up straight away. Rae and I will be delighted to see them.'

I realised for the first time what the expression 'filling up the doorway' meant when Joe walked through ours a few minutes later. And when, with hand out-thrust he enquired, 'Haven't John and Jan arrived yet? They asked us for eight, I smiled sweetly and poured them both a drink, thinking to myself, 'If only I could get my hands around John's neck!'

VETERANS 1, FINANCE 0

I was fortunate in having two outstanding public servants in Pat Galvin and Alan Kerr as Secretary and Deputy Secretary of the Department of Arts, Heritage and Environment. I don't think Graham Richardson had a clue as to what he was losing when he let them go soon after taking over my Department.

Pat retired from the Public Service, but took over as Chairman of the Heritage Commission. Alan transferred to Veterans Affairs as Deputy Secretary.

After almost a year away from Alan, I rang him. 'How's it going, mate?'

'Pretty good,' he replied. 'Just had a big win over Finance.'

'Congratulations, that's a rare one!'

'Yeah,' he said. 'We've got the money for 30,000 extra bed pans and more oil for the wheelchairs!'

THE HOLY HOLE

Monash Country Club, now one of Sydney's leading golf clubs, was established prior to World War II as a social club for Jews who were unable to gain entry to almost all of the leading clubs in the city. As a callow youth of 17, I was fortunate enough to win the Club championship and for a short time held the course record of 69.

So in November 1985, when Deputy Prime Minister Lionel Bowen asked me to deputise for him and present the trophy for the Australian Professional Golfers Association tournament at Monash, I was delighted to accept. That Greg Norman should be the recipient of the trophy made it doubly enjoyable.

When presenting the trophy, I mentioned that I had seen an extraordinary action by a visiting British golfer during the final day's play. The green at the sixth hole had become slippery due to its incredibly steep slope, which resulted in putts hit from the top side literally running off the green. The visitor from the UK, facing a 30-footer downhill and aware of the ball's likely fate, stood looking at it for some minutes almost paralysed with fear. He addressed the ball and froze. Finally he stepped back, looked towards the heavens and crossed himself. With that he addressed the ball again, struck it confidently and watched with shock and horror and, one felt, with a certain loss of faith as the ball careered off the green and almost into the lake.

Only a foreigner would not know that crossing yourself at Monash is a waste of time.

Senator Reg Wright (Liberal Tas) — August 1971
Minister for Public Works
I took the opportunity to travel over this road by road the other day.

SECURITY

My four and a half years as Minister ended in mid-July 1987. Four months later I was made aware of just how close to the bone is the BBC production 'Yes Minister'.

The following letter arrived at my office in Canberra on 4 November.

Dear Mr Cohen

You will recall that as part of a survey of the physical security of the residences of Ministers and office holders an examination was made of your residences earlier this year.

I am attaching for your information the results of the survey of your ACT residence as you may now wish to implement some of the recommended measures yourself.

I will forward the results of the survey of the Gosford residence when the report is received from the Department of Administrative Services.

Yours sincerely,

(D.S. EVANS)
for Secretary

I wondered how long it would be before the Public Service became aware that I was no longer the Minister. The paymaster had certainly found out quickly enough!

MAN'S BEST FRIEND

Ben Humphreys, the Member for Griffith in Queensland, former Government Whip and now Minister for Veterans' Affairs, was in his earlier life a hawker. A noble profession that took him from one side of the country to the other. In a large van loaded with R. M. Williams country clobber, Levi Strauss jeans and saddlery equipment, Ben saw more of the outback of Australia than 99.9 per cent of his countrymen.

One such trip took him to Jubilee Station, just west of Fitzroy Crossing, and tradition demanded that he join some of the managers for a birthday barbecue down on the riverbank where a carton or three of the best Four XXXX was consumed.

The birthday boy, who for the purposes of this story will be known as Mick, consumed his share of the fluid and that of four others. By mid-afternoon, Mick and some of his friends were feeling no pain at all and were unlikely to do so for some considerable time.

It was at this point that the overseer, a man of coarse and uncultured countenance not unknown in those parts, decided that Mick should have a unique experience.

As the poor lad slept the sleep of the innocent, his 'overseer' searched around and without much difficulty located a particularly pungent brand of dog shit. With all the skill of a practised beautician he delicately applied the 'lotion' to Mick's forefingers.

Then, in an act that would have done credit to the Marquis de Sade, he tickled Mick under the nose with a piece of grass.

There are no prizes for guessing what Mick did to stop the itching nose when tickling finally awoke him.

AND THEN THERE WAS ONE

Michael Duffy and I often dined together in Canberra, alternating between Asian delicacies at the Malaysian in Civic and superb pasta at The Village Chef in Manuka. As the evening wore on conversation tended to drift towards the eccentricities and peccadilloes of our Ministerial colleagues. In turn we would recount the latest lunacies of the madder Members of Cabinet, roaring with laughter as we recalled their most recent performances.

One particular evening, as the meal and the conversation

drew to a close, Duffy leant back in his chair, took a long drag on his Willem II and opined expansively, 'Yer know we can all be glad the public has no idea how mad they all are. They cover it up extremely well in public ... generally. When you look at the lot of them, you and I are the only really sane ones there.' He paused, eyes half closed, waiting for my grunt of agreement. After what seemed an interminably long time, during which I had failed to comment, his eyes opened a little and he looked at me directly. 'Well?' he drawled enquiringly.

'Well, I suppose you're right, but then of course you haven't read my next book in which, I tell them about the milk cartoons, I purred in reply.

Rarely have I seen anyone's mood change so dramatically. The mouth dropped and the jaws became slack. The eyes bulged as the cigarillo dropped to the floor and the Minister for Communications, as he then was, sat bolt upright, the colour drained from his face. 'You wouldn't dare!' he screamed so loudly that every guest in The Village Chef ducked for cover, anticipating a hail of bullets.

There was another long pause as I savoured this moment of delicious pleasure. Power is a terrible thing and it can go to your head if you let it. The old expression 'If you've got them by the balls, their hearts and minds will follow' was never truer, as I watched this normal robust individual reduced to quivering jelly. It was not a pretty sight. Duffy's mouth was opening and closing but no noises were coming out. I could no longer stand it. After all he was supposed to be a friend. 'Relax mate, I wouldn't do that, even to Graham Richardson.'

Slowly Duffy's deathly pallor disappeared, his hands ceased trembling and he gradually regained something resembling composure. The subject was never raised again.

Not until now. Having thrown his not inconsiderable debating skills into the Caucus debate in opposition to full-time lump sum superannuation payments to MPs, I feel no obligation to honour that promise, and recalling the reply a prominent journalist gave me when he revealed a conversation he had promised never to repeat ('I'm sorry mate I just couldn't help myself'), I am prepared to reveal why Michael Duffy, now the Minister for Overseas Trade Negotiations, cannot possibly qualify as being described as sane.

Not long after he was elected, a meeting of the Public Accounts Committee was held in Melbourne. Michael invited one of the other members of the Committee, Canberra MP Ros Kelly, to join him for dinner at his home in Parkdale.

After a furtive scour of the kitchen, the Member for Holt bellowed at no one in particular but everyone in general, 'WHERE ARE THE MILK CARTONS?' There was a long silence as Caroline, his wife, and the children looked guiltily everywhere but at father. 'WHERE ARE THE MILK CARTONS?' he roared again, about 20 decibels higher.

After a further long silence as his face changed to a purple hue, his eldest daughter replied tremulously, 'We kept them for you for days and finally there was no more room. They're in the garbage bin.'

'THEY'RE WHAT?' he shouted. 'GET THEM!' Within seconds Alanna had recovered twelve empty milk cartons from the Otto bin and placed them neatly in a row in the lounge-room. The future Minister for Communications' temperature dropped something near to normal. He lowered himself into the lounge chair and grasped the first of the milk cartons. For the next hour, while Caroline prepared dinner, Ros and the children sat transfixed as one of the two 'sane' members of the future Hawke Ministry tore each of the milk cartons into centimetre-square pieces, then placed them in neat piles before returning them to the Otto bin.

Senator Reg Wright (Liberal Tas)
Murder carries a penalty of execution by death.

AND GETTING MADDER

It is not only the family that have to cope with Duffy's strange behaviour. With milk cartons not in over-abundance in Parliament House his fetish is sated by envelopes. A not uncommon sight is to see his rear-end sticking out of the large bins in the House snaffling every used envelope he can find. Once he has acquired sufficient numbers they are sorted into various sizes. The smaller ones are then placed inside the next largest size, which in turn are placed in the next largest and so on until there is only a very large envelope remaining. Duffy finds it difficult to understand why people stare at him when he indulges in this practice. Those who know, understand and sympathise with his problem simply ignore his bizarre behaviour and act as if collecting used envelopes out of garbage bins was standard ministerial behaviour.

Long-serving members of his staff have grown so used to it after five years that they think Ministers who don't collect used envelopes are peculiar. Those staff who have made the mistake of throwing out envelopes have been threatened with the sack or worse.

John Mildren, the Member for Ballarat and Michael's friend, wandered into his office recently with the greeting, 'Are you a member of the Miscellaneous Workers Union?'

'No,' replied Duffy, somewhat perplexed.

'Well you'd better be. The cleaning staff are threatening to go on strike if they see your arse hanging out of the garbage bins any more.'

Fred Daly (Labor NSW) to Sir William Aston (Speaker)
I raise a point of order Mr Speaker. My point of order is that you have already ruled on the point of order, so the Honourable Member cannot take a point of order on a point of order that you have decided is not a point of order.

A STRANGER PASSING BY

No public collecting institution in Australia bears the stamp of one man more than the Australian National Gallery. Although the collection predates James Mollison's appointment by Sir William McMahon in 1971, 99 per cent of the selection we see in the ANG was acquired under Mollison's stewardship. There are few who do not acknowledge that he has done a brilliant job.

On first meeting Australia's Art Supremo, one could easily gain the impression that he was slightly aloof, some might even say patrician. However, as one gets to know James, one realises that the first impression was conservative. Let's face it — he's a terrible snob, particularly with those who don't know so much about art as he does, which rules out about sixteen million Australians. I used to think it was awfully nice of him to accept me as his Minister.

From the moment I took over the Arts portfolio in March 1983, the pressure was on to cut costs. I had to trim back everything, with the result that for a short while relations between us became slightly strained.

When my successor Graham Richardson took over, cost cutting became even more severe. After his first audience with the new Minister, James was told for the fifth year in succession that the Gallery would have to be leaner and hungrier than even he thought possible.

The following evening James had to go to Sydney for an important appointment. Arriving at Kingsford Smith he was surprised to find that instead of the usual Commonwealth car, a reasonably sumptuous Ford LTD, there, standing in all its glory awaiting his arrival was a gorgeous long white stretched limousine. With all the Commonwealth cars booked, the pool had been forced to use the hire car service. Even the normally unflappable James was embarrassed by this apparent ostentation.

With a deep breath he strode manfully towards the

glamorous 'limo'. Only a few steps from his goal he noticed, out of the corner of his eye, his new Minister for the Arts, Senator Richardson. With the style and grace that sets him apart from us normal mortals, James just kept on walking into the night.

Arthur Calwell (Labor Vic)
A point of order Mr Chairman.

Speaker Archie Cameron
I am not the Chairman.

Arthur Calwell
I know you are not but I thought I'd pay you the compliment.

DEAR VOTER

WRAN'S THE MAN

In an article detailing all the problems New South Wales Premier Barrie Unsworth was having in a run-up to an election in 1988 – Darling Harbour, the monorail, Aboriginal protests – *Sydney Morning Herald* journalist Greg Milne quoted Neville Wran's comments to a private gathering at the time of his retirement

'Elections,' he remarked, 'are like erections. You can't make 'em happen. You've got to feel one coming on.'

CHARLIE ME LUD

If there was a competition for the worst festival of the 200 – odd festivals held in Australia each year I would happily nominate the now defunct Central Coast Festival of the Waters and guarantee that it would defeat all challenges.

No festival has been more aptly named. Even during drought-stricken periods the Gosford Shire would be awash for the ten days of the Festival. I'm sure Noah launched his ark during the Festival of the Waters. The only thing worse than the weather were the functions that made up the Festival's activities. Intended to attract tourists it not only failed to do so but inevitably drove the locals out of town. You always knew it was Festival time when the dreaded blow-up Haunted House appeared near the Aquatic Club, surrounded by hot dog and fairy floss stands.

The organising committee seemed somewhat crestfallen as the crowds that had started at zero continued to fall. They needed something dramatic to catch the public's attention. In 1982 an invitation was issued to the Seventh Earl of Gosford to open the thirteenth Annual Festival of the Waters.

Central Coast Society was agog. 'A real fair-dinkum Lord,' fluttered the local society matrons, rushing to their real estate and car dealer spouses to get permission to buy a special gown at Grace Bros. When they heard he was a 40-year-old bachelor it was almost too much. Raelene, Charlene, Valene and Vaseline were also given an extra bath and urged to flaunt their comely wares in front of 'me Lud'.

'Mai daughter Lady Gosford', one could hear them practise under their breath. Were they ever going to laud it (no pun intended) over Mavis at the Golf Club. We'd be hearing no more of Mavis' daughter marrying the bank manager's son!

I was scheduled to meet his Lordship at the opening of the Festival. Probably because of some supernatural prowess on his part, for the first time in thirteen years it wasn't raining. Charlie, as he insisted on being addressed, informed me at our initial meeting that he was coming to Canberra to talk to one of the Parliamentary Committees about an issue that was occupying much of his time in the House of Lords – the health problem of asbestos – and he wondered if I might show him around.

Having hosted a luncheon for him in the Parliamentary dining-room, I invited him to join me in my drive back to Gosford. During our journey I was to hear his most extraordinary story.

The Honourable Charles Acheson was born in England in 1942. His father, Viscount Acheson, had been Air Attaché to the British Embassy in Paris prior to the war. The family fortune having been squandered some generations earlier he, unlike his predecessors, had been forced to work for a living. Hereditary titles for the family went back some centuries prior to the first Earl being elevated to the peerage. An Irish title, the family took their name from Gosford Castle in Country Armagh.

Impoverished by comparison with many of their fellow peers they were, however, able to find the wherewithal to send young Charles to Harrow. Although his fees were paid, he lacked the loose change of his school friends, who nightly visited the town where they dined royally on steak and chips. Charles attributes his spindly frame to the meagre evening fare provided by the school – an apple and a glass of milk.

After leaving Harrow, Viscount Acheson, as he then was, studied art, finally winning a scholarship to The Royal Academy. In 1966, following the sudden death of his father, the shy, introverted Charles became the Seventh Earl of Gosford.

As a struggling artist unable to maintain the lifestyle of his rich and powerful friends, Charles became even more introverted, dropping completely out of sight to become plain Charlie Acheson and undertaking a variety of jobs from truck driver and storeman and packer, to switchboard operator and running a paper delivery service. Years passed and while his two sisters, Lady Isabella and Lady Caroline, married and settled down, the young peer lived in anonymity without any of his workmates suspecting for one minute that a member of the British aristocracy was working beside them. He discovered how the other half lived. By the early seventies, he had decided to resume his artistic career and in time, still as Charlie Acheson, he became secretary of the British Artists Union.

Suddenly, 1977, with the passage of the *Life Peerage Act*, brought about by the action of the famous Left-wing Labour peer Anthony Wedgewood-Benn, Charlie was faced with an agonising dilemma: whether to renounce his peerage or take up his seat in the House of Lords. He had a year to decide.

His agony was caused by the uncertainty of his friends' reaction when they learnt his true identity. It was unlikely that they would treat him as just plain Charlie. At union meeting after union meeting he tried to gather the courage to tell them, but each time his nerve failed him. Finally, with only days to go before the expiration of the date when he had to make a decision about renouncing the title, he bit the bullet. Having decided that there was no appropriate standing order in the union's rules under which he could raise such a matter, he waited until general business had concluded and, with typical British understatement, summoned up the nerve to announce in a whispered undertone, 'I THOUGHT I HAD BETTER TELL YOU THAT NEXT WEEK I PLAN TO TAKE UP MY SEAT IN THE HOUSE OF LORDS!'

There was, as they say, a stunned silence. Nobody moved. Not a flicker crossed the faces of the unionists. The air hung heavy as mouths slowly sagged and the assembly stared blankly at the slight figure of the secretary. Seconds ticked by seeming like hours. Finally a young woman's voice breathlessly broke the silence.
'CHARLIE . . . ARE WE ON CANDID CAMERA??'

(Lord Gosford took his seat in the House of Lords and served enthusiastically for five years, interesting himself in the arts, heritage, product design, and particularly the effect of asbestos on workers' health. He so fell in love with Australia and a delightful eighteen-carat Australian, Lynette, that he decided to apply for permanent residency. Together with Lyn's three children, they live comfortably in an East Gosford home where Charles pursues his increasingly successful career as a painter.

The Labor Party has been accused in recent years of straying too far from its grass roots. Leaders of the Party are accused of spending too much time with industry barons and not enough with workers. I wonder what they would have thought had they passed the East Gosford polling booth in the 1983 elections and spotted the Seventh Earl of Gosford handing out my Labor How-to-Vote cards.)

Geoff Giles (Liberal SA)
The Government in due course acted promptly.

THE ONE THAT GOT AWAY

Arriving in Catherine Hill Bay, a sleepy 'company mining town' just south of Newcastle, one is struck by the last-century appearance of the shabby weatherboard cottages standing in stark contrast to the long sweep of the sandy beaches and the brilliant blue of the Pacific Ocean. Anyone who believes that mining companies are of benefit to the local community need only visit Catherine Hill Bay.

The Village has a special place in my heart because during the four elections I contested during the years when it was part of my seat of Robertson, the polling booth always recorded the highest Labor vote in the electorate. Although less than 300 votes were recorded there, the near 80-90 per cent Labor vote was a nice buffer against booths that went the other way.

During the 1974 Double Dissolution caused by Billy Snedden's refusal to pass the Supply Bills, I was undertaking my usual election day practice of travelling around the electorate to thank the hundreds of booth workers who loyally turned out to work for the Party.

It was late in the afternoon when I finally arrived at the northernmost part of my electorate, armed with the knowledge that the Catherine Hill Bay booth would be in the reliable hands of ex-Police Sergeant Clive Toby, then a milkbar proprietor, and his two female associates. No candidate is ever relaxed on election day and although I thought I would hold the seat, I was unsure of the outcome and apprehensive and tense throughout the day.

Anticipating a warm Labor welcome, I was somewhat alarmed to find the two ladies with looks of consternation on their normally happy countenances.

'How's it going?' I enquired.

'You'd better talk to Clive, they replied in unison, obviously upset by something.

I sidled over to the gnarled old ex-cop. 'Any problems, Clive?' I asked nervously.

'Yeah!' he snapped angrily.

'What is it?'

'A couple came in here a few minutes ago,' he whispered conspiratorially, 'AND THEY TOOK THE LIBERAL HOW-TO-VOTE CARDS!!'

BLUE CHIPP

The Terrigal Red Cross was not known as a hotbed of socialist revolutionary activity. Therefore, as a relatively young MP in a seat previously held for twenty-three years by the forces of darkness, I was more than a little pleased when in 1971, during my first term, I was invited to their Annual General Meeting. Sitting on a margin of 2½ per cent, I needed to make friends in places where those of socialist leanings had normally feared to tread.

So it was that on this fair day, I arrived, albeit somewhat nervously, at the 'luxurious' CWA rooms tucked away behind the old Florida Hotel on Terrigal Beach. It was to be my first meeting with the indomitable Mrs Dangar.

Now, for those who have not met Mrs Dangar and who arrive psychologically unprepared, it can be a daunting experience. It is not an exercise for the faint-hearted. Mrs Dangar eats wimps for breakfast. It is not that she is an unpleasant woman. On the contrary, she is kind and charming. It is just that her voice has a ring of authority that suggests that whatever the subject under discussion, it is not a matter for debate. Mrs Dangar does not speak, she commands. I have yet to meet the person who does not obey.

'Ah, Mr Cohen,' she greeted me at the entrance to the hall. 'Good of you to come. Now we have a small problem.

Our guest speaker has failed to turn up, so if she doesn't come, you'll take her place! You'll speak for twenty minutes and then answer questions!'

I was left open-mouthed and twitching as the tweed-suited figure of Mrs Dangar disappeared across the other side of the room, arranging seats, organising afternoon tea, selling raffle tickets and generally instructing the fifty-odd Terrigal ladies in their Red Cross duties.

What in God's name was I going to talk about? Still in my apprenticeship, I was not yet confident enough to turn up and make a major speech without thorough preparation. While Mrs Dangar conducted the Annual General Meeting, I racked my brains for subject matter and nervously looked out for the missing guest speaker.

It was a shame in many ways that my mind was not totally in focus on the events unfolding before me. Not surprisingly, no one questioned the President's report. In fact, when she bellowed 'Any questions?' I thought we were having a minute's silence for the dearly departed.

This was followed by an exercise in democracy that would have made Genghis Khan proud. It proceeded as follows:

MRS DANGAR: Nominations for President?
VOICE: Mrs Dangar
MRS DANGAR: Thank you. Nominations for Secretary?

A short silence followed before she turned to the frail, diminutive figure quivering beside her.

MRS DANGAR: What's wrong with you?
SECRETARY: I can't!
MRS DANGAR: Why not?
SECRETARY: (With quavering voice.) My daughter's having a baby.
MRS DANGAR: Good God, woman, it only takes nine months

and she's having it, not you. You'll do it! Now, Nominations for Treasurer?

And so it proceeded until all positions were filled. Mrs Thatcher would have been proud of her. With the democratic niceties dispensed with, Mrs Dangar turned to me.

'Well now, our guest speaker has failed to appear, so Mr Cohen's going to do the honours . . . Ladies . . . Mr Cohen!'

'What would you like me to talk about?' I whispered to her.

'I heard you rabbiting on in Parliament about censorship the other day, so you can give that a go.'

I looked closely at her to see if she were pulling my leg. Don Chipp, Minister for Customs and Excise in the Gorton Government, after almost a decade as an arch-conservative, had suddenly taken an interest in pornography. Kinkiness knows no political boundaries. Suddenly he had become the darling of the small 'l' liberals and the *bête noire* of the pursed lips set. After years of strict censorship you could suddenly hear and see people saying s . . . and f . . . on the screen. It was Chipp's contribution to Australian culture. To convince the more timid among the pollies, Chipp had arranged two special showings of what he had cut out of the movies.

It was, as I recall, a sellout night at the National Library. Instead of having to sit through hours of boring movies just to catch the salacious and titillating bits, the politicians were able to get the choicest selections from twenty-nine movies in just one hour. I had the rare experience of sitting between two of the identities of the Federal Parliament, who were there no doubt, purely for research purposes, one E. G. Whitlam and the late Senator Vince Gair.

The second of the 'Blue Chipp' showings were two films, one from Canada and one from Sweden. The latter showed explicit lesbianism and group sex scenes that had a dear old woman member from the New South Wales Legislative

Council, who was sitting in front of me, alternatively hiding under the seat or groaning, either from disgust or ecstasy.

Chipp's exercise in liberalising censorship seemed to set him on a new course that made him the darling of the middle-class trendies who eventually formed the Democrats.

It impressed those who didn't know his past record as a kangaroo-culling, pro-conscription, pro-Vietnam War Right-winger. Still, they say, a week is a long time in politics.

To his credit, the liberalisation was long overdue, and with Mrs Dangar's request ringing in my ears, and looking at the demure collection of twin-sets, tweed skirts and blue rinses in front of me I thought, 'Why not?'

I spoke for twenty minutes. I described in minute detail the excerpts from the twenty-nine movies and as delicately as I could, the Canadian and Swedish movies. The talk covered sex, violence, sado-masochism, rape, adultery, group sex, lesbianism and a few practices that I had not even heard of.

When I finished I sat down exhausted. No one spoke. The silence was exquisite. All you could hear were fifty elderly ladies breathing, and breathing very heavily. Finally Mrs Dangar cleared her throat, stood up and asked in a high-pitched voice (for her), 'Any questions?'

The words were hardly out of her mouth when half-a-dozen ladies leapt to their feet and with but one voice screamed, 'WHEN ARE YOU COMING AGAIN?'

ALIVE ON TV

The Hon. John Norman Button (Leader of the Government in the Senate and Minister for Industry, Technology and Commerce), may be one of the shortest leaders in our history, but he has the longest title in the Hawke Government. A lawyer by profession, but nevertheless an honest man, he had not been long elected to the Senate (1974) when he was elevated to the front bench as Shadow Minister for Communications during Gough Whitlam's twilight zone (1975-77).

Whilst one could hardly describe a 40-year-old as childlike, he was at this period in his life a sweet, innocent and trusting soul, despite a reputation to the contrary.

So it was that during the 77 election campaign, he generously accepted the invitation of the Western Australian branch to undertake a tour of the sand belt in support of Labor's candidate for the largest democratic seat in the world, Kalgoorlie.

Arriving in Geraldton, he was greeted warmly by the locals, who informed him that the newly opened television station was promoting his appearance on TV that evening.

'We hope to see you this evening,' they told him.

'What do you mean, you hope to see me?' he asked.

'Well, we don't watch to see what's on, but whether it's on. It keeps going off the air.'

It was not a confident Shadow Minister who arrived at the tin shed that was the television studio in which he was to make his TV debut in Geraldton.

The newsreader, who was to interview John later, sat behind the obligatory desk, while the diminutive Senator was seated in a cane chair, replete with artificial pool, beach umbrella and palm trees.

'After the news,' the announcer intoned, 'I will interview Senator John Button, ALIVE IN THE STUDIO!' John nodded approval. Half way through the news, the announcer announced, 'We will now pause for a commercial break.'

The producer waved his arms frantically, whilst mouthing the words, 'NO COMMERCIAL'.

By now, our newsreader was starting to lose his cool.

'There will be no commercial break. Instead I'll read the last item again.'

Finally, the news ended and a commercial break was

taken. The announcer leapt out of his chair and in his multi-faceted role, grabbed a long pole and embarked on a rampage around the studio, belting the spotlights into submission, or at least until one shone halo-like on the Shadow Minister for Communications. Seconds to go before the interview, John suddenly heard a choking cry from the announcer.

'SENATOR,' came the stage whisper, 'THE MIKE.'

'The what?' cried the startled Button.

'THE MIKE!' he screamed. 'IT'S UNDER YOUR CHAIR!'

John reacted with the speed of an athlete. And so it came to pass that as the good burghers of Geraldton tuned in to watch the most important interview in the short history of Geraldton TV, the first view of Senator John Norman Button, Shadow Minister for Communications in the Whitlam Opposition, was, as he groped beneath the cane chair for the mike, a wide-angled view of his arse.

Ultimately, the picture improved as he settled back in the cane chair for a long interview. The questions were good, although the interviewee noticed that his host occasionally referred to matters that were a few years out of date. The Broadcasting Control Board had, for some time, been called the Broadcasting Tribunal. John made a note to tackle him about it afterwards.

The interview ended and, after shaking hands, they both started to walk off the set. This brought a startled reaction from the producer, who once again went into the dance of the whirling dervish as he waved his hands in desperation.

'THE WEATHER!' he screamed. 'THE WEATHER!'

'Oh, shit!' snarled Geraldton's answer to Brian Bury, realising he had forgotten his weather notes.

'SORRY, FOLKS!' he waved at the audience. 'NO WEATHER TONIGHT!'

By now the startled Senator was wondering what was going to happen to him next. He thanked his host for the interview and pointed out some of the errors he had made.

'Well, I'm sorry, I am a bit out of touch. You see, I've been in jail for the last three years. They only let me out to do the news!' John's eyes widened.

'Yeah, as a matter of fact, that's why we had to finish by nine o'clock. I've gotta be back inside by 9.15!'

THE PERFECT CANDIDATE

Having written a manual for candidates titled *A Winning Campaign*, and been successful in holding a marginal seat for many years, through good times and bad, it was not surprising to be called upon by both the State and Federal Campaign headquarters to help in election campaigns.

On the eve of a very important by-election, I received a panic-stricken call from a Party organiser, asking for my help.

'What's the problem?' I asked.

'Well . . . er . . . the problem is that we haven't got a very good candidate. He's short and ugly and he fights with everyone. We want you down here to see if you can polish him up a bit,' the organiser replied.

'I must confess,' I replied, 'that's not a very good start. Can't you keep him out of sight and just have him making statements and the occasional speech?' said I.

'Well, that's another problem,' shot back the obviously harassed official. 'He doesn't understand Labor policy. He keeps making up his own policies as he goes along.'

'Look, surely you can go through the policies with him and explain what they are, what he should say and what he shouldn't?'

'Well, that's another problem. He won't listen. You can't tell him anything.!'

'For God's sake, man!' I cried, getting quite irritated by his negative approach. 'Give him the policy papers and tell him to study them and stick to them!'

There was a long silence on the other end.
'Are you still there?'
'Yes,' a plaintive voice replied.
'Well?'
'You're not going to believe this,' the voice croaked.
'Try me!'
'He can't read,' he sobbed.
'I'll be right down!'

ALL HIS OWN WORK

Tony Doyle, the young member for Peats who replaced Paul Landa when he died so tragically, was having the usual problem that Labor members seem to have at election time with someone defacing his posters by painting obscenities all over them.

These mindless acts of vandalism were duly reported in the local media, to the embarrassment of the Liberal candidate, Dennis Swadling. Within hours of the brouhaha about the posters, an irate Liberal supporter rang Mr Doyle's campaign headquarters.

'It's alright for you Labor people to complain about your posters being defaced, but what about what you've done to Swadling's posters!' he shouted.

'I'm sorry, but I don't know what you're talking about,' replied Joy Groves, Tony Doyle's secretary.

'Drawing moustaches on all his posters!'

'I don't understand.'

'You understand all right. I know you Labor thugs!' he shouted.

'We didn't draw anything on Mr Swadling's posters,' replied Joy. 'HE HAS A MOUSTACHE!'

MAKE MY DAY!

Tony Sansom, for many years my electorate research officer, was Labor's endorsed candidate for the State seat of Gosford in the March 1988 election. State Premier Barrie Unsworth had angered the gun lobby by introducing tough new gun laws. Fortunately it was not the issue in the Gosford area that it was in some rural electorates, where huge meetings of the gun lobby were held.

Nevertheless, Tony received some calls from irate gun owners who saw their manhood threatened by the loss of their second most prized possession. One such personage arrived at his campaign headquarters at Green Point to inform him that he had no intention of voting Labor at the forthcoming election because of the new gun laws.

Tony patiently explained to the angry individual that the reason the Government had acted was due to the increasing incidence of domestic violence that had resulted in husbands shooting wives and vice versa, quite often with the children being killed as well.

'Listen, mate,' explained the angry voter, 'I've been working in this area for years and quite often that's the only way to resolve the problem!'

OFF WITH THEIR HEADS

The Royal Surf Carnival at Terrigal during the Bicentennial visit of Prince Charles and Lady Di was surely the biggest event in the history of this normally quiet tourist village.

I have never seen so many socialist republicans, including 'Lady Rae' and myself, at a Royal event. Still, there was a State election in the offing and it doesn't hurt to be seen near 'you know who'.

Thousands lined the beach and the main street to get a butchers at the Royal couple as they watched the most traditional of Australian summer sports on a glorious summer's day. No effort was spared to ensure that everything went without a hitch.

The Royals must have thought we were going just a little too far to make them feel at home when over the PA system came the following announcement: 'Here's another little blonde girl who has lost her parents. She's in a floral swimming costume, so if anyone sees her, bring her over to the tower!'

I wonder what they thought we do to serious offenders?

Senator Sir Magnus Cormack — June 1970
I have had three attempts [at dairy farming] and I have lost money on every one of them. I claim at least to know something about dairying.

Senator Sir Magnus Cormack — Nov 1971
President of the Senate
Questions without answers — I mean without notice.

LIFE WITH GOUGH

SEND IN THE CLOWNS

There were many who suggested that there were so many Gough stories in my first book, *The Life of the Party*, that it would have been more appropriately titled 'Life with Gough'. Naturally I had sent him a copy, and was anxious to get his impressions, but at the time of its release he was reluctantly overseas fulfilling responsibilities that were a legacy from his period as Australian Ambassador to UNESCO.

Arriving at the Ansett VIP Lounge in Canberra, I was delighted to see his huge frame tucking into delicacies provided for guests.

'Comrade!' he cried. 'Just the person I wanted to see!' He advanced towards me, cheese in one hand, pâté in the other. 'Have my solicitors been in touch with you about my share of the proceeds of the book?'

'So you've read it?' I enquired.

'I've read the important bits. I checked the index! Well done!'

Having passed the ultimate test, I relaxed and we chatted about matters of State.

'Let's arrange to sit together,' I suggested, only to find on examination of our boarding passes that we already had adjoining seats. Suddenly he dived into his inside top pocket and pulled out a small pocket diary, opened it and, after checking something on his boarding pass, wrote some numbers in the diary. 'What are you doing?' I asked.

'It's a hangover from days as a navigator,' he replied, referring to his wartime service in the RAAF. 'I keep a logbook. It's important that historians know where I was at any particular time.' He looked down at me imperiously with a twinkle in the eye and the self-mocking half smile that is his unique trademark.

I tried not to laugh. 'As a matter of fact,' I said, 'one of the great regrets of my life is that I didn't keep a proper diary of my twenty years in politics. Did you?'

'No!' he sniffed, looking pensively towards the heavens as if seeking communication with an equal. 'I was too busy making history to record it!'

This time I could no longer contain myself. 'God, you're a funny man!' I laughed. 'If I could just follow you round for a couple of months I'd have enough material for another book.'

'FUNNY!' he bellowed. 'FUNNY? Witty, yes. Epigrammatic perhaps, but not FUNNY!' He looked wounded. 'You make me sound like a clown.'

LOOK MUM — BOTH HANDS

Shortly after assuming the Prime Ministership, Gough was invited to open the historic Lachlan Village at Forbes. Prominent radio journalist John Tingle was among the vast entourage of media personalities who accompanied the PM. Still enjoying widespread popularity, Gough found himself surrounded by a throng of local ladies wherever he went. Spotting John, he sidled over and whispered in his ear, 'I'm busting for a piss. Where it it?'

'Unfortunately, Prime Minister, the project is not completed yet, so they've erected some emergency accommodation,' explained Tingle as he pointed to the hessian stalls erected some distance away.

The Prime Minister set off at a gentle trot, determined not to upset the balance of nature, but followed by the blue rinse set of local ladies. It took some convincing by local officials to allow the Prime Minister to continue with his allotted task without all the 'camp-followers'.

The 5-foot hessian wall was not really sufficient to hide the 6-foot 5-inch frame of the Nation's leader. Crowds walked past silently, fascinated by the sight of the Great Man, eyes watering, but staring stolidly ahead.

Not so one young child, who excitedly exclaimed to her parent, 'Look Mum, there's the Prime Minister!' Excitedly she waved nonstop to the unblinking Gough.

'Why doesn't he wave back?' she cried sadly.

'Both hands are busy,' replied a gnarled old rustic who happened to be passing.

ENCORE

He had only just become the first Labor Prime Minister for twenty-three years when he was invited to be the Guest of Honour at a girl's high school in the Sydney suburb of Cronulla. Normally such a relatively insignificant function would not have attracted the attention of the Leader of the Nation. Edward Gough Whitlam, however, was a man aware of the historical and spiritual significance of his roots. It was from Cronulla, a part of the original seat of Werriwa, that he had commenced his journey on the road to the Lodge.

Hundreds of young ladies of delicate sensibilities and their teachers awaited his address. As they did so, they were all entertained by a concert that finished with a dance sequence by a gaggle of young nymphs dressed in diaphanous gowns, trailing silk streamers behind them. After a particularly spirited performance, they rushed forward en masse and, to thunderous applause, collapsed on the ground in front of the podium where our glorious Leader was ensconced.

He rose as in a mystical trance, stepped to the microphone and spoke.

'Headmistress, Ladies and Gentlemen, Girls. I normally lay them in the aisles, but it doesn't usually happen until after I have spoken . . .'

FRANKLY SPEAKING

Charlie Jones, a former boilermaker, MP for Newcastle and Minister for Transport in the Whitlam Government, could never have been mistaken for the new breed of look-alike, Zegna-suited young executives who now dominate Labor politics. 'Old school' in style, manner and temperament was the phrase that quickly sprang to mind whenever he hove into view.

This makes the following exchange between the plain-speaking Minister for Transport and our former glorious Leader, after one of Charlie's submissions had been debated in Cabinet for over four hours, so fascinating.

GOUGH: Jones, this is a shithouse submission!
CHARLIE: And you're a shithouse Prime Minister . . . so why don't you go to the shithouse?

A PUFF OF WHITE SMOKE

In an interview with Lord Chalfont on the BBC, Gough had replied to a question as to whether he was a Christian by describing himself as a 'fellow-traveller'.

The subject of religion had come up for discussion during a Cabinet meeting, whereupon Gough announced, 'If I were a believer, I'd be a Catholic.'

'Yes, and you'd start as Pope, no doubt!' snapped Bill Hayden.

A CLASSLESS SOCIETY

In an attempt to stem charges of profligacy, the Whitlam Government decided that it would practise self-denial by having MPs and senators fly economy class instead of first class. Minister for Transport Charlie Jones was far from impressed and in his usual shy, retiring manner informed Cabinet of his views on the matter.

'This,' opined Charlie, 'is the most stupid bloody decision this Cabinet has made. Ministers are putting in a hundred hours a week as it is, and one of the few opportunities we get to work is on the plane. Now we won't even be able to do that in comfort!'

The Prime Minister, it appeared, had somewhat different views about some of his Cabinet colleagues.

'Most of the people around this table are pissants, and they can travel first class for the rest of their lives and they'll still be pissants. I, on the other hand, could travel economy class forever and still be a great man!'

ONE BLUE TO ANOTHER

Gough at a banquet given by the Lord Mayor of London in December 1974: 'I'm told, my Lord Mayor, cricket is not the game in which you excel, nor is it the one in which I do. You were a rowing blue, I'm told, and I was some such myself. It is, of course, an extraordinarily apt sport for men in public life, because you can face one way while going the other.'

ON THE LINE

David McNicoll, columnist for the *Bulletin* and many other Sir Frank Packer publications, was not known for his espousal of the Socialist cause. I can recall one of my colleagues saying of McNicoll that whilst he couldn't stand the right-wing ranting that appeared in McNicoll's columns, he always read them to 'find out what the top end of town was thinking'.

A handsome man with prematurely white hair and a

distinguished moustache to match, one felt that he had stepped straight out of an advertisement for an expensive brand of Scotch whisky. His literary style did not quite match the foppish air he exuded.

Gough was in his office one day when the phone rang.

'Hello?' spoke the Leader.

'David McNicoll here, Prime Minister. I'm speaking for Sir Frank...'

'David!' gasped Gough, 'I didn't think you ever did anything else?'

NOTHING'S CHANGED

During the Whitlam Government's term in office, a request was received from a Dr Kuntz seeking access to material from the National Archives on the policy of the Federal Government, in the immediate postwar period, regarding its treatment of European doctors. Many had migrated to Australia with extremely high qualifications but had been refused permission to practise medicine in Australia because of the rigid rules of the British Medical Association (BMA), the forerunner of the Australian Medical Association (AMA). Some of Europe's finest medical minds were forced to take low-paying, menial jobs because of this arrogant and restrictive practice.

Lots of agonising went on in the Departments of Prime Minister, Health and others before the submission to the Prime Minister recommended against giving Dr Kuntz access to the files. However, the final decision was one for the Prime Minister.

The submission was returned with the following written in the margin by Gough:

'LET HIM HAVE THE PAPERS. IT WAS THE BMA, NOT THE GOVERNMENT WHO WERE THE KUNTZ!'

This being right at the height of the Nixon Watergate

scandal, 'KUNTZ' was crossed out by the author and the words 'EXPLETIVE DELETED' substituted.

WHAT EVER HAPPENED TO . . .?

With one of the periodic reshuffles that marked the Whitlam Government in the offing, Senator Reg Bishop (South Australia) had heard rumours that he was to be moved from Postmaster-General to Police and Customs. Having already been shifted from Repatriation to Postmaster-General, he was apprehensive that, having just settled into his new job, he would have to go through the trauma of learning a third. In a panic he rang his colleague, Lionel Bowen, who at the time was Special Minister of State and Minister Assisting the Prime Minister.

'Mate,' he said, 'you've gotta do something for me. Speak to Gough! I don't want another change.'

Bowen had only just finished speaking to Bishop when he received a call from 'Above'.

'Bowen,' spake the man himself, 'come up here. I want to show you the changes I've made to the Ministry.'

Lionel entered the inner sanctum to find the Prime Minister deep in discussion with the Permanent Head of his Department, John Menadue.

'You're just in time, Comrade. Read him the list!' He waved at his Permanent Head, as he leaned back in his armchair with the smug expression of one well satisfied with his work.

'You're moving to Manufacturing Industry,' he informed Lionel, making it clear it was not a subject for debate.

'And Daly's going to be Postmaster-General.'

Bowen stiffened as he realised that it was too late to save Bishop and listened as Menadue read the names of the new Ministers off the back of an envelope.

'Hayden . . . Treasurer, Morrison . . . Defence, Cavanagh

... Police and Customs.' Bishop was certainly going to have his worst fears realised. 'Daly ... Postmaster-General and Administrative Services,' and so on.

The list completed, Gough looked at his new Minister for Manufacturing Industry with eyebrows raised, anticipating his approval. Bowen said nothing.

'Well, Comrade?' intoned the Great Man.

'What have you done with Bishop?' enquired Lionel innocently.

There was a short, pregnant silence. Nobody moved. Suddenly Gough leaned forward, grabbed the envelope from Menadue's hand and scanned it intensely.

'BISHOP! ... BISHOP!' he bellowed. 'WHERE THE F. . .ING HELL IS BISHOP?' His teeth were grinding by now at full pelt.

'You'd better leave him as Postmaster-General,' opined Lionel.

There was an even larger pause as Gough realised there was no one else to vent his anger upon.

'Yes,' he muttered through what was left of his back teeth as he wrote, 'BISHOP ... POSTMASTER-GENERAL!'

SEVEN OUT OF TEN

Travelling from Perth to Sydney one day, I found myself on the same plane as our former Leader. Having just completed what I thought was a particularly fine speech for a forthcoming address on racial discrimination, a subject I knew was dear to his heart, I passed him a copy with the comment that I thought he might find it interesting.

Twenty minutes or so later, he came striding down the aisle, sat down beside me and handed me the speech. Each of the sixteen pages had been carefully corrected for spelling, grammar and punctuation, and there were numerous notations in the margins suggesting I check various Acts, conventions and speeches to ensure accuracy. I turned to the last page to see what mark I had received out of ten.

I was not the only one to have been 'corrected' and 'marked' by the 'headmaster'.

David Connolly, Liberal Member for Bradfield and a member of the Coalition's front bench under both Andrew Peacock and John Howard, reported to the Parliament an exchange of views between His Excellency, the Ambassador to UNESCO, and himself.

MR CONNOLLY (BRADFIELD): Madam Speaker, I seek your indulgence to correct an error which I made during my contribution to the debate on the Protection of Movable Cultural Heritage Bill in this House on 17 February.

MADAM SPEAKER: The Honourable Member may proceed.

MR CONNOLLY: I am indebted to Australia's Ambassador to the United Nations Educational, Scientific and Cultural Organization, Mr Whitlam, who phoned me at 8 am on Saturday, 1 March, to point out the error of my ways. He said that while he was not interested in what Liberals said on anything — I am delighted that he made an exception in this case — nevertheless, he was concerned that my error could damage Australia's relations with Greece. In deference to our Ambassador, I doubt that his Greek colleague in Canberra would read *Hansard* with the same fervour as evidently he does, or that he would think my error was more than Antipodean ignorance.

During the debate, when commenting on the celebrated case of the Elgin marbles which were taken from the Parthenon by Lord Elgin, I said that he was Ambassador to Greece. Of course, that was incorrect and I apologise for the error. Lord Elgin was Ambassador to Constantinople, which at the time included a very unwilling Greece within the Ottoman Empire. Despite the early hour, I am indebted to Mr Whitlam for waking me up and I enjoyed our extensive tour-de-horizon, which included his visit to the Roman ruins along the Algerian coast, a quick sortie across to Rome to comment on the quality of the Vatican's post-graduate degree in archaeology and finally a pithy analysis of the First Crusade . . .

ACCORDING TO ST GOUGH

I had heard that on the release of the massive tome *The Whitlam Government, 1972-75* Gough was asked by an intrepid young reporter whether this was the third major work on his period of government, the others being *The Truth of the Matter* by himself, and *A Certain Grandeur* by Graham Freudenberg. He was reported to have replied loftily, 'Yes, there was the Crucifixion, the Resurrection and now we have the Gospels.'

I had tried to check the authenticity of this wonderful story with the man himself but was unable to do so as he was away overseas for a considerable period, fulfilling his UNESCO obligations.

I eventually caught up with him and repeated the story. He paused for a moment before replying, 'I must say I can't recall it, although it has a certain ring to it. However, I can tell you that I do keep 'THE THREE BOOKS' together on my office shelf.'

'The three books?' I enquired innocently.

'Yes,' he replied, *'The Bible, The Complete Works of William Shakespeare* and *The Whitlam Government!'*

THE HUMBLEST OF THEM ALL

It was at the gala spectacular to launch Neville Wran's Sydney Entertainment Centre that Australia's speechwriter extraordinaire, Graham Freudenberg, bumped into his former boss, Gough Whitlam. After a quarter of a century of writing speeches for successive Labor leaders, Graham was now dividing his time between writing for Bob Hawke and Neville.

'Comrade,' Gough enquired confidentially, 'what's it like, in the biblical sense, serving two masters?'

'Well,' replied Graham hesitantly, 'there's not really any problem ... except perhaps that Neville always sticks strictly to the text while Bob tends to wander off on his own from time to time. I suspect he believes he can speak better than I can write.'

'Yes, Comrade,' said Gough, 'I understand your problem. THE MAN'S GOT AN INSUFFERABLE EGO!'

THE MEEJA

AFFIRMATIVE ACTION

The following article appeared in the American publication *New Republic* on 8 June 1984. It will have a familiar ring to anyone in Government who, in recent times, has had to put together a Committee.

Fairness Democratic Style

Preferences
Be it resolved that the Democratic National Party shall, during the 1984 Democratic Convention, create the Fairness Commission which shall be responsible for the review and revision of the Democratic Party Rules . . . The Commission shall consist of at least 50 party members equally divided between men and women, and shall include fair and equitable participation of Blacks, Hispanics, native American, Asian/Pacifics, women, and persons all of sexual preference consistent with their proportional representation in the party — resolution adopted by the Democratic Party — Rules Commission.

Okay, let's see . . .
 Twenty-six women and twenty-four men.
 Twenty Blacks, fifteen Hispanics (five Puerto Rican, five Mexican, five other Latin), five native Americans, ten Asian/Pacifics. What? Oh, right. So make it ten whites, take five from the Blacks, three from the Hispanics and one each from the native Americans and Asian/Pacifics. No sweat.
 Ten gays, thirty-five straights, three celibate/onanists, and two pedophile/beastiophile/miscellaneous. Beastiophile? Note to liaison staff. What is a value-free term for animal lovers? Check with Humane Society.
 Thirteen who prefer the lights on and thirty-seven who prefer the lights off.
 Twenty-four at night, twenty in the morning, six between noon and 4 pm.

Thirty-one, one partner or less, twelve two, seven three or more.

Twenty-seven on top, twenty-one underneath, and two standing up. What? You're kidding? Well, if Yankelovich says so, eight on top, twenty-nine underneath and thirteen standing up.

Eighteen rock, eleven classical, twelve Country-and-Western, five jazz, nine 'All Things Considered'.

Fourteen a cigarette afterwards, ten a long walk, nine an old movie on TV, eight a shower, six chocolate-chip icecream, three cab fare home.

Fifty who prefer no sex at all to any cuts in Social Security.

Michael Kinsley

LIBERATION THEOLOGIAN

The following advertisement appeared in the *Manchester Guardian* on 1 April 1986:

LIBERATION
THEOLOGIAN

The Theologian will be responsible for initiating, developing, administering and conducting studies aimed at combating capitalism, monetarism, neo-colonialism, fascism (including body fascism) ageism and other indefensible modes of behaviour which may come to light as the work proceeds. The person selected will be serviced by a multi-ethnic research team including not less than 15% lesbians and gays. He or she will have the services of a Principal Ethics Officer whose duties will include the placing of liberation in a theological context. A working knowledge of divinity, though desirable, is therefore not essential to the appointment.

Salary 25,427 pounds +; four and a half day week; protective clothing, and use of unmarked van.

Auditions will be conducted at the Cottesloe Theatre from May 3-9.

Applications, enclosing birth certificates and C.V., should be addressed to the Clerk to the Overseer, County Hall, London. SE1, marking envelope 'Leviticus'.

WOMEN HEALTH WORKERS

Sydney Morning Herald, classified advertisement 15.11.86:

> Women Health Workers

Wanted for feminist abortion clinic in Harbord. Experience not necessary but bilingual nursing, herbal or bookkeeping skills helpful. Aboriginal and migrant women encouraged to apply . . .

AN AFFAIR OF THE HEART

Laurie Brereton was treated cruelly by Premier Barrie Unsworth when he was made the scapegoat for the Government's unpopularity over Darling Harbour, the Monorail, the proposed Harbour Tunnel and, in general, what my dear friend Jim McClelland described as the Government's 'edifice complex'. Leaving aside the Monorail, I believe history will show that the Wran-Unsworth period in office was marked by some of the most visionary redevelopment in the State since the time of Governor Lachlan Macquarie.

Apart from the above there has been the construction of desperately needed facilities such as The Entertainment Centre, Chinatown, Darling Harbour, Parramatta Stadium, the Powerhouse Museum, Sydney Cricket Ground, Sydney Football Stadium, Mt Tomah Botanical Gardens, Homebush Bay Bicentennial Park and many others. As Minister for Public Works and Ports and Minister for Roads, Laurie played a key role in making many of these projects become a reality. Some, such as the Monorail and Darling Harbour, went through periods of temporary unpopularity for which

Laurie had to take the dump. As they became unpopular, so did he. He was, however, not shy of identifying the name Brereton with these projects.

One Sydney radio commentator, who had just recovered from major heart surgery remarked, 'Laurie Brereton has his name on every by-pass in Sydney, but mine'.

A SEAT BY ANY OTHER NAME

Shortly after I was elected to the House of Representatives for the Seat of Robertson in 1969, I raised the question of the suitability of the name of the electorate. The seat, which had covered over a third of the State at the time of Federation, had shrunk to the Central Coast region from the Hawkesbury River to Lake Macquarie.

I pointed out that while Sir John Robertson may have been a notable person during the latter part of the nineteenth century, history had not been kind to him, and most people in Australia were totally unaware of his name or his place in Australia's history.

I suggested that the seat should be named Kendall, after Australian poet Henry Kendall, who had lived for many years in the area where he had written his famous poem 'Bellbirds'. The cottage where he lived had been preserved as a museum and a local high school had been named after him.

Within days of my speech a letter appeared in the *Sydney Morning Herald*, asking who was this brash young whippersnapper who had only just arrived in Parliament and already was besmirching the good name and distinguished career of one of Australia's greatest citizens. The letter detailed Robertson's long political career, pointing out that he had held many important ministerial positions, including Premier, in the New South Wales governments of the latter half of the last century, and had been responsible for the introduction of the 'free selectors' legislation. The letter was signed 'Mrs Agnes ROBERTSON'.

Although my later research was to lead me to agree with his great-grand-daughter, that Sir John had in fact been a very distinguished servant of the people and in his time quite a radical reformer, I still took the view that Kendall would be a more appropriate name. When the Whitlam Government was elected I renewed my campaign with the new Minister responsible for electoral matters, my old friend and mentor, the lovable Fred Daly.

One day when I was pestering him once again about a name change, Fred's patience gave out and he offered me a bit of sobering advice.

'For God's sake stop worrying about the name of the damn seat. It doesn't matter what they call it, so long as you hold it!'

THEY WALK ALONE

I well remember shaking my head in disbelief when Kathy Lette of *Puberty Blues* fame described to me her experiences at a women writers' seminar.

Those present decided that the event would no longer be referred to as a seminar, because the word 'seminar' had male connotations. Instead, the conference would be known henceforth as an 'ovular'. I understand from Kathy that from then on the level of discussion deteriorated.

It is good to know, however, that in Australia we are not alone. 'The Forces of Light' are alive and well back home in the mother country, as the following item in the Diary Column of the *Manchester Guardian* of 4 August 1984 shows:

OH! The tortuous moral dilemmas faced by those in the vanguard of medical science. Older readers will recall the ethical problems confronting Ms Ann Flowers, a member of Brent South CLP (Constituency Labour Party) when she decided to get pregnant by trying both artificial insemination as well as another lover (a Labour Party branch secretary) while simultaneously living with Graham ('the social father'). Ann shared her affections and fears with readers of London's *Labour Briefing*, to whom she returns in the July issue with the next chapter of her life.

Ann is no celibate, but still determined to become pregnant by 'self-insemination'. 'One of the questions I had to face,' she writes, 'is why I was looking for a white man to provide sperm. Was it a form of racism to want a white child, was it racism to want a child of mixed race?' Ann has eventually settled for white, but now she asks herself: 'Why am I living in an all white women's house? Not having a child of mixed race reflects the fact that my whole cultural, living arrangements are 'white'.'

But Ann has no doubts about self-insemination itself: 'I think it challenges the idea of biological links as the basis for a relationship between adult and child . . . It deals a blow at the power of the biological father.' The things Mary Warnock never thought of . . .

REVERSAL

Clive Robertson on 'Newsworld' in late 1987 announced: 'The Queensland National Party today reversed its decision on condom vending machines . . . They put condoms in and get money out!'

Senator Bob Cotton — May 1971
Minister for Civil Aviation
I don't know when the report will be made available. When it is available it will be made available.

AROUND THE HOUSE

SUDDEN LOSS

I had served with one of the Coalition Members for a number of years on a Parliamentary committee. Knowing that he was not one of the great intellects of the Parliament, I was more than a little surprised when he was suddenly appointed to the Ministry. I sent him a telegram congratulating him, only to hear a few days later; that his wife had died.

The following day I found myself standing beside him in one of the Parliamentary urinals, not the most elevating place to carry on a conversation, but the first opportunity I had had to sympathise with him over his sad loss. 'Yes,' he remarked wistfully, looking skywards, 'it took a bit of the gloss off the appointment.'

THE BROADSIDE

The Marine Science Bill that set up the Australian Institute of Marine Science was debated in the House of Representatives on 17 May 1972.

THE LEADER OF THE OPPOSITION, MR WHITLAM: . . . I quote what was said on the fifteenth of May by a new Minister for the Navy [Dr Malcolm MacKay], of perhaps a different calibre from his predecessor.
MEMBER FOR MORETON (JIM KILLEN, FORMER MINISTER FOR THE NAVY): Larger or smaller?
WHITLAM: The new man is of lesser calibre, but a bigger bore.

> **Dr Jim Cairns — April 1971**
> In a sense this statement means anything, it means everything, and it means nothing.

THE CALL OF THE WILD

The late Eddie Ward is, to many old Labor stalwarts, the epitome of the working-class battler. Member for East Sydney (1931-63) and Minister in the Curtin and Chifley governments, he was, according to colleagues he served with, a tireless worker and one of Parliament's most aggressive speakers.

In full flight one day, Eddie was interrupted by an extremely loud noise. One of his Labor colleagues, Rowley James, had 'broken wind'. Without missing a beat, he turned to the Hansard reporter and enquired, 'did you get the Member for Hunter's interjection?'

NO LAUGHING MATTER

Bert James, son of Rowley James and Member for Hunter (1960-80), former policeman and one of the real characters of the Parliament during my time in Canberra, was in full cry during the debate on the Crimes (Aircraft) Bill late in the evening of 26 September 1963.

A giant of a man, almost as wide as he was tall, Bert had a booming voice and a grand sense of theatre. It was not unknown for him to cause an uproar when fully wound up. Throwing books, papers, roaring, crying and a range of other antics and emotions were all part of Bert's oratorical armory.

Unlike many of his colleagues on the far Left of the ALP he was an ardent advocate of capital punishment. He used the bill before the House of Representatives to press the case for the death penalty by giving examples of hideous crimes that he had been familiar with during his long career in criminal investigation:

... after murdering the young man and ravishing the young lady, he placed the dead body of the man in the car, set fire to the car and pushed it over a cliff. Indisputable evidence of these facts was presented at his trial. He was sentenced to life imprisonment and two or three years ago he was found dead in his cell in Maitland gaol. While in gaol he had to be kept under constant surveillance by warders. It is strongly rumoured that while in gaol, on one occasion he held another prisoner's head in a vice in a workshed and committed sodomy on him!

At this point his Labor colleague, the mild-mannered Member for Mitchell, John Armitage, interjected, 'I suppose that's what they call getting your vice-versa!' The House erupted with laughter, to Bert's great annoyance, and he turned on the hapless Armitage and roared at him, 'It's allright for you to laugh! It wasn't your head in the vice!'

SECRET WEAPONS

Ten years in the House of Representatives does not qualify you for the veteran category, but you have reached the point when you can proffer advice to the newcomer. One thing I did suggest to new arrivals was not to make the mistake of interjecting when Jim Killen was speaking. Those who failed to heed this very sensible piece of advice invariably finished up winning that week's 'Egg on the Face' award.

Regrettably, I occasionally failed to listen to my own special brand of wisdom. Anyone who is familiar with cartoonist Larry Pickering's annual lurid calendars of famous national figures, stark naked with extraordinary appendages, will understand why I would have been wiser not to have attempted to interject during Jim Killen's answer to a question from Michael Hodgman (Member for Denison).

MR HODGMAN: My question is directed to the Minister for Defence. I notice in a publication entitled *Pickerings Playmates* that today is the Minister's birthday. Does the enhanced new look of the Minister for Defence as advertised in the 1979 Pickering calendar, herald a new era for the defence forces? Can they, as shown by the example set by the Minister, expect newer, bigger and better equipment?

MR KILLEN: My attention was drawn to this publication. When I first saw it I thought that all my birthdays had come at once. I was greatly impressed and enormously flattered. I thought that it was quite the kindest thing that had happened to me in the whole of 1978. There is an observation made by Chaerephon in Plato's *Charmides* to this effect on seeing the undraped male figure: 'my, it makes one forget the face'. I have to be honest about it and acknowledge the fact that it was my face. As for the equipment, I must say — in envy, mark you — that I suspect that in radically refurbished form, the equipment belongs to the honourable member for Robertson.

MR COHEN: Mr Speaker, I have been misrepresented grievously. I ask for a withdrawal.

MR MALCOLM FRASER: I ask that further questions be placed on the Notice Paper. With your indulgence, Mr Speaker, may I say also that the honourable gentleman who asked for a withdrawal knows perfectly well that it is within his own capacity to demonstrate whether or not he was misrepresented.

WHOOPS!

Entering the Parliament one day on the House of Representatives side, near my ministerial office, I bumped into an old friend whom I had met in the 1970s during my university studies at the Australian National University (ANU).

A former Serjeant-at-Arms in the House of Representatives, he had departed in the late 1950s to take up an academic career, first at Adelaide University, then ANU, before moving to the University of Western Australia where he became Deputy Vice-Chancellor and Professor of Politics.

'Hi! How are you?' I cried, delighted to see him after so many years.

'Very well,' he replied, 'and congratulations on making the Ministry.' We chatted amiably about this, that and the other before I finally asked, 'And what are you doing with yourself in Western Australia these days?'

'I'm the Governor,' replied Gordon Reid.

PERKS

Having decided that this would be my last term in Parliament, I spent many months going through nearly twenty years of correspondence sorting out what I wanted to keep and what could be appropriately forwarded to the Archives. I came across this little gem:

17 July 1985

Dear Member,

PARKING — MACQUARIE UNIVERSITY, NORTH RYDE

For some time an entry fee of sixty cents has been levied on vehicles entering to park in the grounds of Macquarie University.

The Registrar of the University has advised this levy will no longer apply to Members of Parliament who either advise the University in advance of their visit, or make themselves known to the gatekeeper.

Yours faithfully,

(LYN SIMONS)
Acting Serjeant-at-Arms

THE TIP OF THE GOLDBERG

The Hawke Government and Dr Neal Blewett, the Minister for Health, caused an uproar in many sectors of the community and the Jewish sector in particular, when they announced that in the future, circumcision would not be eligible for a Medibank rebate. Like many Jewish laws, it had been initially introduced thousands of years ago as a health measure and, through observance, had become an essential part of Jewish law. It had only been in recent times that non-Jews had adopted the practice. The latest fad among sections of the medical profession is to claim that it is not a desirable health measure and to recommend against it.

Few MPs agonise more over the problems of their constituents than the wonderfully warm and emotional Jeanette McHugh, who represents the one seat in Australia, the Bondi-based seat of Phillip, where the Jewish vote can determine the result. Frantic about the impact of the Government's decision, she was not comforted when the following telegram arrived from her colleague Colin Hollis, at that time the Member for Macarthur and now the Member for Throsby: 'ALARMED AT THE DECISION OF GOVERNMENT TO DISALLOW CIRCUMCISION AS MEDICAL BENEFIT. THIS IS THE UNKINDEST CUT OF ALL!'

THELMA'S BACK

When electorate staff were sick or on holidays, it was the practice of the Department of Administrative Services to provide a replacement from the pool of relief secretaries available to them.

I arrived at work one morning at my office in Carbow Arcade to be greeted by one of the regular 'pool' secretaries, who for the purpose of this story will be known as 'Thelma'. A handsome, albeit comely woman, she was the epitome of the staid, reliable, responsible secretary.

'Mr Cohen, would you mind if I used your office for about an hour?'

'What for?' I asked innocently.

'Well, I'd like to strip off and lie down beside the radiator.'

I knew I shouldn't have asked and I was also aware that I was short of a good follow-up question. 'Thelma' had obviously noticed that while my mouth was open, not much sound was coming out. Before I could formulate the word 'Why?' she answered blandly, 'Oh, I spent the weekend shagging and I've done my back in. The heat will do it the world of good!'

Senator George Georges (Labor Qld) — September 1971
Could I ask you, Mr President — what is the function of Senator Marriott?

President of the Senate, Sir Magnus Cormack
Order! Senator Marriott is a Senator sitting on my right.

Phil Lucock (Country Party NSW)
Chairman of Committees
I did not give a ruling that I did not give a ruling.

AROUND THE WORLD

FAMILY REUNION

Through the combined efforts of the Melbourne Jewish community and the Israeli Government, delegations of politicians from the major political parties have visited Israel in recent years.

The first of these groups, visiting in January 1983 prior to the election of the Hawke Government, included six MPs who were later to become Ministers: John Brown (Sport, Recreation and Tourism), Barry Jones (Science), Ben Humphreys (Veterans Affairs), Ros Kelly (Defence Science and Personnel), Senator Robert Ray (Home Affairs) and yours truly (Arts, Heritage and Environment), Ross Free (Member for Macquarie, now Lindsay) and Secretary of Caucus. Sergio Sergi, who was to become my Senior Private Secretary, made up the delegation.

Australia to Israel via Los Angeles and London is a long and exhausting plane trip, so by the time we had arrived at Ben Gurion airport, it was not surprising that tempers were a little on edge. After a blazing row with one member of our delegation, I stormed across the tarmac to the VIP lounge with the Australian Embassy official who had been sent to meet us. I could see no sign of members of my family who live in Israel and whom I was expecting to be there to meet me.

'Where are my uncle and aunt?' I roared at him.

'I beg your pardon?' stammered the young man.

'My Uncle Jules and Aunty Suzie! I sent a cable to you to tell them the time of our arrival and the flight number!' By now my temperature was rising to near boiling point at this 'stupid boy'.

'I, er, . . . I'm sorry I didn't, er, know about them, er, what's their name and, er, where do they live?'

I could stand this idiocy no longer. How could anyone be so thick?

'MR AND MRS COHEN!' I screamed. 'TEL AVIV!'

CLOCKING OFF

During the 1983 tour of Israel that I had organised and led, Barry Jones and I, unaware that in a few short weeks we were to be Ministers in the Hawke Government, were strolling down Disengoff Street in Tel Aviv, accompanied by the only genuine cosmopolite among us, Sergio Sergi, who was acting secretary to the group before becoming my Senior Private Secretary and later Interim Director of the National Maritime Museum.

No evening with Barry and Sergio is ever dull and the excellent dinner that had preceded our stroll was no exception. With so many beautiful women around it was not surprising that the subject came up for discussion. Barry mentioned that he had never been terribly successful with the opposite sex. A long discussion had taken place in which I pointed out that if he had any problem, it was largely of his own making.

'Actually,' I said, 'some women find you very attractive but you don't seem to take a lot of interest in women, as women.'

Barry's eyes widened to the size of dinner plates. 'What do you mean? Of course I'm interested in women!' he protested strongly.

'Yes, I know that' I said, 'but you don't show it and you don't show them. You don't look as if you're the slightest bit interested in them as women. You walk around in Tel Aviv of all places, where you see some of the most beautiful women in the world, and you seem oblivious to their presence!'

Barry seemed troubled by our comments and refused to accept the points we were making. He was adamant that we were talking nonsense. By now we had arrived at the Tel Aviv Hilton and were strolling along the boulevard, gazing at the exclusive fashion and antique shops that were there to cater to those with a lot more money than our poverty-stricken group.

At that moment, an extraordinarily elegant and beautiful young Israeli girl walked out of the foyer of the Hilton and sashayed down the footpath towards us. Sergio and I stopped dead in our tracks. Our jaws went slack, our eyes bulged as we stood mesmerised by this stunning Semitic beauty. 'Barry,' we both hissed, 'DID YOU SEE THAT?'

'Of course I did!' snapped Barry impatiently, looking back towards the antique shop. 'An outrageous price for a Tiffany clock!!'

THE GREAT LEAP SIDEWAYS

The old saying that 'there are none so blind as those who don't want to see' was never truer than when applied to those idealogues of the Left who made the compulsory visit to China during the reign of Mao. The hospitality, courtesy, honesty and the friendliness of the Chinese people blinded visitors to the dreadful backwardness of the country after a quarter of a century of Communist rule.

The great egalitarian experiment, where everyone worked for the good of their fellow man, loved their neighbours and thought of nothing but disarmament and peace, was music to the ears of old Australian Lefties who had suffered for so long under the oppression of the neo-colonialist, capitalist bourgeoisie and their running-dog lackeys.

The sight of simple peasants working in the fields, living in their humble abodes and satisfied with little more than a bowl of rice, whilst building a Socialist Utopia, stood in stark contrast to the pampered decadence of the three-bedroom, red-brick, two-garage, TV-owning, sun-loving Australians they had left at home. If only Australians would realise what they were missing!

As they, themselves, were wined and dined nightly on

eighteen-course banquets which of course was a standard Chinese nosh-up, particularly if you had the 'right' political views, they were held spellbound by fascinating stories about how the Chinese had eliminated flies and prostitution. Anyone who suggested that perhaps the reason the 'gels' were off the streets was because no one could afford them, was put down with a withering stare reserved for deviationists.

One of the earliest delegations to visit the People's Republic consisted of just such a group of enlightened, progressive Labor MPs and Senators. Included in the delegation was one of the best minds in the Parliament, Senator John Wheeldon.

To say that John was less than impressed by stories of 'The Great Leap Forward' was to put it mildly. He felt as he inspected the Dickensian factories and the country club-style communes, that life 'Down Under' was bearable.

His colleagues, however, would have none of that. After inspecting their fifth commune in as many days, they stood in the fields gazing longingly at their utopian dream.

'Amazing,' gasped a leading member of the group, breathlessly.

'What?' enquired the puzzled Wheeldon.

'This!' he replied as he waved his hands majestically at the open grasslands whilst the others nodded approvingly.

The future Whitlam Minister peered intently across the vacant farmland, trying to ascertain precisely what it was that impressed his three comrades. A lone brick outhouse broke the monotony of the arid wasteland.

'I'm sorry, but . . . I, er . . . can't see anything.'

'This!' shouted the irritated MP, as he repeated his imperious wave at acres of grass. 'Look what they've been able to achieve AFTER ONLY 30 YEARS!'

THANKS FOR THE MAMMARY

The Left Wing of the Australian Labor Party has always claimed to be the conscience of the Party. A bulwark against those opportunists on the Right who would sell out their principles to gain power, they exuded a 'holier than thou' aura that the 'pragmatists' on the Right found somewhat irritating.

In the late 1960s, two of the Left's finest, Senator John Wheeldon and Dr Jim Cairns, future Ministers in the Whitlam Government, were under incessant attack from everyone on the Right, including their own party, the Liberal and Country parties and the DLP and its guru, Bob Santamaria, who ran the National Civic Council and published the often vitriolic *News Weekly*.

During their anti-Vietnam campaign, John and Dr Jim found themselves in San Francisco at the commencement of a tour of the United States. With a free evening they decided that an after-dinner walk around the city would assist their digestion.

After an hour or so of window shopping and gazing at the wondrous sights of the licentious 'Frisco, they decided a mild libation would do neither of them any harm. It was only after they had seated themselves at the bar and ordered drinks that they realised that an inordinate amount of attractive flesh was bounding around before their eyes. The Conscience of the Party had inadvertantly wandered into a topless bar.

After a few minutes, when their eyes had come back into focus and their jaws had snapped shut again, the effervescent Wheeldon chortled to his partner, 'This wouldn't look too good back home, eh, Comrade?'

The taciturn Cairns stared at his friend for a while and then finally spoke. 'It'd look pretty good on the front page of *News Weekly*!'

A REMARKABLE LIKENESS

One of the most enjoyable trips Rae and I have ever had was travelling round Australia with Paul and Tricia Eddington. Paul had just completed ten months in Australia in *HMS Pinafore* and had a couple of weeks to spare before returning to England to do another series of 'Yes, Prime Minister'. It was our pleasure to show them, their son Hugo and his girlfriend Geraldine the best that Australia had to offer.

Our first stop had been in Townsville where Paul had done a series of TV commercials for the Great Barrier Reef Marine Park Authority, and we had decided to drive the 250-odd kilometres to Cairns and the Daintree before going on to Kakadu National Park and Ayers Rock and the Olgas.

We paused in our journey north at a pleasant little cafe at the seaside town of Cardwell. Having finished our meal, Paul went to the counter to pay the bill and was greeted warmly by a very affable gentleman who turned out to be the owner.

'Enjoy the meal?' he asked.

'Oh, very much, thank you,' replied Paul, his English accent quite unmistakable.

'English, are you?' enquired our host. 'Having a good trip?' The conversation went on in the same vein for a few minutes with the usual pleasantries being exchanged. 'Gee, you Poms produce some great television. D'yer ever watch a show called "Yes, Prime Minister"?'

'Oh, occasionally,' replied Paul.

'Well, I hope you don't mind me saying so, but you sure look a dead ringer for the bloke who's in it!'

'Really?' said Paul.

KIRK WHO?

Bernard Archer is a reasonably well-known actor who has appeared in a number of BBC television programs. His problem is that he bears a striking resemblance to Kirk Douglas. The result, not surprisingly, is that he constantly has people coming up to him saying, 'Excuse me, Mr Douglas, but may I have your autograph?' He has lost count of the number of times he has had to explain to people that he is not Kirk Douglas.

Travelling by plane one day, he noticed two women across the aisle constantly muttering to each other and looking rather nervously at him. Eventually one summoned up enough courage to come over and ask for his autograph.

Rather than go through all the usual rigmarole of explaining who he wasn't, he thought 'What the hell!' and promptly signed the book 'Best wishes, Kirk Douglas'.

A few minutes later he overheard the lady who had got the autograph mutter somewhat disappointedly, 'That's funny, I would have sworn blind that was Bernard Archer.'

THE NIGHT TRAIN TO BOMBAY

Nigel Hawthorne, better known as Sir Humphrey Appleby from the 'Yes, Prime Minister' series, was in India for the filming of the award-winning film *Gandhi*. With a few days break from work, he was able to travel around the countryside a bit and see some of the sights. Before doing so, he decided to check with the booking clerk at New Delhi Railway Station.

'What time does the train to Bombay depart?' he enquired of the Peter Sellers look-alike.

'At 8.15 pm,' replied the courteous, smiling clerk.

'And it arrives . . .?' enquired 'Sir Humphrey'.

'Oh, yes!'

(From the *Bulletin*)

THANKS TO THE RAJ

India is not the only country in the world where they regard 'Yes, Minister' as a serious documentary, but it is the only country where it is an understatement.

There are a number of prerequisites for anyone making their first visit to the sub-continent. Allow, first of all, for an extra three days in your vacation for filling out forms. That way you'll see all you intended to and also master calligraphy.

The culture shock starts before you leave the plane. The embarkation form is just marginally less complex than the Australian tax return. I am still trying to fathom why some Indian public servant wants to know my late father's name. I am sure that looking down from above he will be delighted to know that somewhere deep in the bowels of the Indian National Archives it will be recorded that Louis Cohen's son visited India fourteen years after he had departed these earthly shores.

After 200 years of the Raj the British boasted that whatever mistakes they may have made they had bequeathed their brown brethren an efficient public service administration. One wonders what they would have considered a failure.

Bureaucratitis is an infection and the disease has spread from the Raj-inspired public service to the private sector. On booking into the Imperial Hotel (where else) I bequeathed my life story to the impassive clerk at the reception desk. Returning twice with my wife and two sons during the next eleven days I was, despite my protestations, required to provide him with two reprints. Should I ever decide to write an autobiography I shall merely seek to requisition my cards from the Imperial Hotel. Incidentally, protesting is a waste of energy in India. No matter how hysterical you become, and I was on the fringe almost daily, the Indian official, private or public, can make the Chinese look positively animated.

With the internal problems India has had with both the Sikh and Tamil independence movements I have no complaints about the Israeli-like security system at the airport. However, Australian/Indian relations were nearly severed as I watched the security guard stare blankly as my son Adam's newly acquired sitar slid gracefully off the conveyor belt and crashed on to the concrete floor. With my wife near tears, and yours truly not far behind, I went through the useless ritual of lodging a complainant.

'Not to worry, Sir. You will get the glue and stick it together,' was the not unexpected advice. It will be a long time before Adam makes a return visit to India.

Arriving, leaving, booking into and out of hotels and cashing travellers cheques are all rich experiences not to be missed (not that you could miss them) during one's visit to India. They are, however, nothing compared with the joy of making a phone call. Telecom officials should select their ten top complainants and give them a ten-day free holiday in India on the understanding that all their internal arrangements will be made by phone.

It all started when we left behind a parcel at the Moghul Sheraton Hotel in Agra. Arriving later than evening in Jaipur, some 250 kilometres west, I mentioned casually to the reception desk clerk that I would like to speak to the management at the Sheraton in Agra.

'No problem, Sir,' was his confident reply. Twenty-four hours later I would have liked to ask him what he thought a problem would be like.

After three failed attempts over a four-hour period I was finally called to the phone during dinner. Ten minutes later I staggered back to join the family like a stunned mullet.

'What happened?' asked Rae.

'Don't ask me to explain what I've just been through because I couldn't. All I know is that the final word from someone was, "I am being very sorry Sir, but there is no one here". No doubt the five hundred guests and staff at

Moghul Sheraton had all gone out for the night. I re-booked the call for eight in the morning, confident that a good night's sleep would prepare me for another attempt.

I was under the shower when I heard the phone ring. Knowing that Rae, during our courting, had been a super-efficient telephonist-receptionist, I relaxed, confident that she could handle any situation.

Still drying myself ten munites later in the bathroom, I was surprised that no sounds were coming from the bedroom.

'Are you alright dear?' I shouted. Silence. Stepping out I spied the dear gel staring glassy-eyed into space.

'What happened?' Still no reply.

Finally she spoke. 'I don't know,' she said.

'What do you mean, you don't know?'

'For ten minutes I've been shouted at by at least four other people. The trouble is I didn't know if I was speaking to our hotel operator, their hotel operator, the exchange operator or the manager of the Moghul Sheraton in Agra.'

'What did they say?' I asked gently, realising she was in a delicate state.

'I don't know', she stammered. 'Finally I screamed "STOP ... PLEASE SPEAK ENGLISH!" and after a long silence someone replied "I AM!".'

'Then I said "TO WHOM AM I SPEAKING?" and after another long silence he said "You are speaking to ME madam".'

AFRICAN SAFARI

The Australian Parliamentary delegation to Africa in July 1982 was led by the then President of the Senate, Senator Harold Young (Liberal SA), and included Senators Robert Hill (Liberal SA), Kerry Sibraa (Labor NSW) and members of the House of Representatives Leo McLeay (Labor NSW), John Moore (Liberal QLD), Stephen Lusher (National

NSW) and yours truly. It was to be an eventful trip as we cut a swathe across the Dark Continent which left a trail of devastation behind us.

I should have realised that the stars were in the wrong position when the three Labor Members were recalled from overseas for the first of the Hawke-Hayden clashes. Having missed the Nigerian and Somalian legs of the tour we rejoined our colleagues in Kenya before visiting Ethiopia, Zimbabwe, Zambia and finally Mauritius.

A more peaceable group than this magnificent seven would have been impossible to find, yet where ever we went there was trouble. Hours before our arrival at Victoria Falls the hotel we were booked into was robbed and the clerk at the reception desk was killed. The following day, just 30 kilometres from where we were staying, six young tourists, including two Australians, were kidnapped by rebel forces and tragically never seen again.

All this was just a preliminary to the main event. Having been joined by our wives for the last leg of the tour we returned to Nairobi prior to having a three-day break, at our own expense I might add, so that we could visit the game parks of Kenya.

Hours after our departure for different regions, Nairobi was aflame as a result of an attempted coup. Almost 400 people died as the Air Force attempted to take over the city. It was a very nervous and sweaty group of delegates that dribbled back into the burned and looted capital after three days of wondering what was to become of us.

Despite the jinx we seemed to bring to whichever part of Africa we were visiting the delegation was welcomed warmly by Prime Ministers Robert Mugabe (Zimbabwe), Kenneth Kaunda (Zambia), and Presidents Mengitsu (Ethiopia) Moi (Kenya) and Banana (Zimbabwe). It's hard to believe but that's his name — Dr Joseph Banana, President of Zimbabwe.

Among his many claims to fame he has attracted considerable attention by continuing to play competitive soccer at the age of 40. The former residence of the Governor of Rhodesia was now the Presidential palace and a delightful old colonial mansion it was, set in superb lawns and gardens. Whilst the delegation chatted with the President about affairs of state and his athletic prowess, Mrs Banana invited Yvonne Sibraa, Cherie Lusher, Janet McLeay and Rae to inspect her pride and joy, the vegetable garden.

After the magnificent splendour of the front of the Palace the ladies were less than impressed by the weed-encrusted garden. Rae, always the diplomat, was unable to restrain herself.

'There's a few days good weeding here for the President,' she informed Mrs Banana.

Unabashed, the First Lady of Zimbabwe then escorted her guests to the chicken house. After the appropriate clucking noises of approval concerning the state of the Presidential poultry the ladies were more than a little surprised to find, neatly laid out in a line outside the chook house, six dead rats.

'The man who looks after the chooks always likes to show me how many rats he's caught each day,' said the President's wife, totally unfazed by the look of stunned amazement on the ladies' faces. Even the 'First Lady' of Robertson was unable to think of an appropriate reply to that one.

With that, Mrs Banana triumphantly led her guests back to join the men. As they were about to re-enter the Palace they were forced to duck their heads under the washing line where eleven yellow soccer shirts flapped merrily in the breeze. Unable to contain herself yet again the good lady wife inquired, 'Why so many soccer shirts?'

'Oh, my husband's team,' replied Mrs Banana casually, 'and it was my turn to wash the sweaters.'

Senator Keith Laught (Liberal SA)
Nauru has an indentured workforce. That is to say the workers are indentured.

Kim Beazley Snr (Labour WA) — September 1970
In Papua New Guinea the trade unions can put in claims until they are black in the face.

OUR MAN IN . . .

NAUGHTY GIRLS

One of the responsibilities Australia accepted after the independence of Papua New Guinea was to represent them in a number of countries where they could not afford a Mission.

So it was that Sergio Sergi, later to be my Senior Private Secretary, but at the time First Secretary in the Australian High Commission in Hong Kong, was asked to go to Tak airport to meet a Government Minister from PNG.

The Daimler was parked on the tarmac as the plane from Bangkok taxied along the runway. The plane door opened and out stepped the Minister, wearing only a straw hat and a Bangkok Sheraton Hotel towel. In his hand he carried a small string bag with a radio cassette.

Without batting a diplomatic eyelid, Sergio enquired, 'Minister?'

'I went to de brothel and de girls stole all my clothes,' grinned the Minister, as if no further explanation were necessary.

Sergio bundled him into the Daimler and they sped off to the Mandarin Hotel, easily one of the best hotels in Hong Kong, if not the world. There was more than mild surprise as the pin-striped, double-breasted diplomat and the informally attired Minister tripped lightly through the foyer of the Mandarin.

Reception clerks, if they choose, can be rather forbidding characters to those whom they think are beneath them. It was therefore not surprising that the duty clerk looked down his nose at the apparition appearing at the main desk.

'Yes?' he enquired haughtily. 'May I help you?'

'Yes,' said Sergio, who can outsnob the best of them when he chooses, 'I believe you have a room for the Minister from PNG.' The clerk raised one eyebrow and looked at the betowelled politician as if someone had farted.

'And who is guaranteeing the bill?' he enquired loftily.

'I am,' replied Sergio, matching the clerk eyebrow for eyebrow.

'And who are you?'

'I'm SERGIO SERGI,'' he replied, and then paused, 'from the AUSTRALIAN High Commission.'

This was too much for the clerk, who was used to almost anything. His hand went up like a traffic policeman. 'I'll get the Manager!' he croaked as he disappeared.

After some phone calls to the Australian High Commission, the Minister was finally installed in his room and Sergio was able to relax.

The next morning a cable arrived from the Embassy in Bangkok: 'Tell the Minister his Wassermann test is positive.'

Later, when Sergio had to perform this unenviable task, the Minister laughed heartily. 'Oh! Those naughty girls!' he squealed, unabashed.

SIR 'BERT' PATTERSON

When I first started travelling abroad as an MP, I was struck by how 'Anglicised' were our Foreign Affairs Officers. With their private school background, accents, dress and manner, they were almost indistinguishable from the Brits. That started to change in the late 1960s and 70s as pressure forced Foreign Affairs to widen its net and accept applicants to their cadet training scheme who had attended ordinary public schools. The system became so egalitarian that even a few 'wogs' and 'jews' got in, something quite unheard of in early times.

It was during this period of rashness that my future aide Sergio Sergi was accepted. His meagre qualifications included a BA (Hons) Adelaide, MA (Cantab.), majoring in English literature, and fluency in seven languages.

I had arrived in Mexico City in January 1980 as Shadow

Minister for Sport, Recreation, Tourism and The Environment and had been invited by Sergio to attend a private Australia Day party at the house of one of the Embassy staff. Pies, cocktail sausages, lamingtons and pavlovas were in abundance for the Australian staff and their guests from other foreign posts. Liberal quantities of Fosters were imbibed to capture the full spirit of Australia Day.

Leaning up against one of the walls clutching a tinny in one hand and a meat pie in the other was a character whom I will refer to as 'Bert'. The beer gut, the bowling creams and sandshoes together with a certain air of nonchalance as he held up the wall enabled me to make an accurate guess that 'Bert' was an Australian. I was wondering how this lad had managed to gate-crash the party.

'I see you've met,' said Sergio with an amused look. I wondered what was going on.

'You two know each other?' I enquired, quite surprised.

'Sure,' said Bert, 'we work together.'

'Oh,' said I, 'and what do you do?'

'I'm the Consul.'

I couldn't help it. It just came out. 'You're f...ing joking!' I choked.

'Nope,' said Bert quite unfazed, 'been Consul for a couple of years.'

'Shit!' I said. 'I thought you were Secretary of the Wallabadah RSL.'

NEIGHBOURS

Among Bert's duties was the processing of migrant applications. Now Mexico is not a major source of migrants for Australia, nevertherless our Embassy did receive a steady stream of applications for immigration, and a number of these were approved regularly.

Sergio had noticed that for the past three months not one application for immigration had reached his desk. The fact that it coincided with Bert being given responsibility for processing migrant applications had not escaped him. He called him into his office. The following enlightening conversation took place.

'Bert?'

'Yep!'

'I noticed that there haven't been any applications for immigration coming across my desk.'

'Nope!'

'Aren't we receiving any applications?'

'Yep!'

'Well, what's happening to them? Are there any problems?'

'Oh, no!' he replied languidly, 'I just ask myself the question "Would I like this bastard living next door to me in Canberra?"'. Bert paused, 'so far the answer's always been NO!'

Sergio looked at Bert for some time, lost for words. Finally he recovered his composure.

'Bert, using that as a yardstick, my father wouldn't have been admitted to Australia.'

There was a further long pause before Bert replied, 'NO!'

SEÑOR BERT

Bert's special talent was that no matter how many years he spent in a foreign country, he was completely unaffected by the culture, language or lifestyle.

On Sunday morning a frantic call from the Mexican authorities informed our First Secretary, Sergio Sergi, that a young Australian couple had been tragically killed in a bus accident in Oaxaca (pronounced *Wahaka*). As the town had no mortuary, the bodies were being kept in the local meatworks. The authorities therefore requested the quickest possible disposal. Bert, our intrepid Consul in Mexico City, was despatched by Sergio post-haste to resolve the problem.

Within hours of seeing him off at the airport, Sergio received a call from the agitated Bert.

'What's the matter?' enquired Sergio.

'NONE OF THESE BASTARDS DOWN HERE SPEAK ENGLISH!' moaned Bert.

OUR MAN IN MEXICO

Bert was at his best when assisting distressed Australian visitors. The Australian embassy in Mexico City received a phone call one day from the Mexican authorities, informing them that they were holding a young man in Guadalajara and were intending to charge him with possession of drugs. Sergio immediately despatched Bert there to see if he could give the young fellow any assistance. It turned out that the man had been held in custody in appalling conditions for the previous four months.

Within hours of Bert's arrival, Sergio received a panic-stricken phone call from the distraught Australian.

'Listen mate, do me a bloody favour will you? Don't send that bastard down here any more!'

'Why? What did he do?' asked Sergio.

'What did he do!' shouted the near hysterical caller. 'He gave me a lecture on drugs. Told me it was all my own fault. Said it served me right and told me I'd be lucky if I ever got out of gaol. Jesus, I was in a bloody mess before he turned up. After his visit to cheer me up, I wanted to slash my wrists!'

HIS EXCELLENCY

It was a wet Saturday morning in Mexico City and Sergio had only just returned from the Embassy's office to his home, a block away from the Ambassador's residence, when the phone rang.

'Sergio?' It was the Ambassador. 'I need you down here immediately!' he snapped with an air of authority that indicated that it was not a matter for debate.

'There goes my Saturday afternoon!' thought Sergio as he gathered up his umbrella and headed off to do his master's bidding.

A few minutes later he stood outside the residence, feeling somewhat overdressed for a Saturday afternoon, in his dark pin-striped suit, with brolly held aloft. A few seconds later, when the door opened, he felt even more overdressed. Standing before him was His Excellency, the Australian Ambassador to Mexico, dressed in a frogman's suit and flippers. 'Follow me!' he cried and set off up the stairs with Sergio at his heels.

As the Ambassador, in full underwater regalia, flip-flopped across the roof of the residence, followed closely by his senior officer in formal attire and brolly in the pouring rain, Sergio mused at what sort of picture they must have made to the neighbours. He half-expected to hear sirens wailing.

They came to the edge of the house where it was obvious that His Excellency had been cleaning out the gutters.

'Look!' he shrieked hysterically, pointing vaguely towards the South Pole. Sergio followed the general direction of the trembling arm, trying to focus on precisely what it was that was disturbing the Ambassador. There was a long pause as Sergio tried frantically to find an answer. The problem was he didn't even understand the question.

'Er . . . I'm sorry Sir, but I don't understand. What exactly is the problem?'

'That!' shrieked the Ambassador.

'Sir?'

'That tree!' he bellowed, pointing at a large tree outside the Embassy wall, with one overhanging branch. 'Can't you see what a security risk that is?'

By now Sergio was convinced that his superior, whom he had always thought was more than a little eccentric, was a shingle or two short.

'Er, I'm sorry . . . er, Sir, but I er . . . I'm not sure what you are getting at,' stammered Sergio in his best diplomatic manner.

By now Our Man in Mexico City was nearly apoplectic. Spluttering with rage and nearly purple in the face he shouted at his First Secretary through gritted teeth, 'Can't you see that some terrorist might shin up that tree, climb along the branch, drop down on to the residence and try to assassinate me?'

There are occasions when one would pray for a lead-in like that. Sergio was mute. The offending branch was removed the next day.

THE PARTY AT PLAY

JOINING THE PARTY

When I informed the bride in early 1964 that I was joining the Labor Party, you would have thought I had just informed her that I was a child molester.

'He's gone Commie on us!' she would tell our friends and look at me with the supercilious air one usually reserves for the lowest of the species.

A few days earlier, a white-haired man, with the loosest fitting dentures I had ever seen, had called at our house in Galston Road, Hornsby Heights, to inform me that he had received a message from the State Secretary Bill Colbourne that I was a prospective new member. The sucking and slurping required to keep his teeth in, interrupted intermittently by the castanet-like sounds of his dentures, made it difficult for me to understand his description of how to get to the meeting of the Hornsby branch. I finally got him to write the address on a piece of paper.

I left the peach brick house we were renting and set off with a great sense of excitement tinged with ideological fervour, as I took my first step towards solving the world's manifold problems. Less than an hour later I was back.

"Blow up any bridges tonight?' said the supportive one.

'Smart arse!' I snarled.

'I thought it would take you at least two hours to become Premier,' said she of the jolly countenance.

'If you want to know, I couldn't find the bloody place!'

I didn't mind her laughing, but why did she have to do it with such obvious glee.

'You couldn't what?' she screamed with delight. 'Sir Winston Cohen couldn't even find the place. The man who was going to lead us out of the darkness into the dawning of a new era?'

She reads too much.

By now she was clutching her sides trying to stop them from splitting. I was looking at the paper with all the addresses on it.

'Oh, Gawd,' said I. 'The place I went to was the secretary's address in Wahroonga. The meeting's being held at the Railway Institute.' The Revolution would have to be delayed another month. In the interim we had another visit from he of the badly-fitting dentures, wanting to know what had happened to me. I explained, somewhat shamefacedly, my navigational error and promised faithfully that I would be present at the next roll call. I mused as to what they might do if I failed to appear for the second meeting. Probably denounce me as a running-dog lackey of those following the bourgeois capitalist road and send me off to the Gulag.

Rather than start on the long, cold journey to Siberia, I made sure that I was at the branch meeting place and on time as well. It shouldn't be difficult to find Labor Party branch meeting places. Simply look for the dirtiest, most depressing and draughtiest public building in the district.

It is not an accident that it is thus. It is part of a carefully prepared plan by the Party hierarchy of both the Left and the Right to keep the Party small. If they can't find it, they can't join. If they can't join they can't vote you out of the exalted position you hold as assistant secretary of the Hornsby, Gulargombone or Grong Grong branch of the Party.

Eventually, I discovered the Hornsby Railway Institute in the month of April in the year of our Lord 1964. There, gathered in those hallowed precincts that certainly had not seen worse days, was a jolly bunch of honest workers who had assembled to listen to the then New South Wales Minister for Transport, John McMahon, deliver a paean to the State's transport system. It should have been one of the shortest speeches in living memory, but he somehow managed to ramble on, Castro-like, for almost an hour, explaining why less and less people were using the Government's trains and buses. When he finally finished, I realised that I knew less about the State transport system than when he started. I was totally confused, if somewhat relieved that his dissertation had concluded. Or so I thought. The Chairman then used a phrase I was to come to dread over the next twenty years: 'Any questions?'

This is supposed to be the part where I thought people would seek further enlightenment. Silly me! Initially there seems to be a reluctance by those present to ask questions. Just when you think there isn't going to be any and we can all go home, or at least get on to General Business, the first question comes. It appears that everyone feels obliged to ask a question that is either banal in the extreme, or has absolutely nothing to do with the subject under discussion.

Eventually all good things have to come to an end and the meeting was over. The smart, the intelligent thing to do would have been to tuck my head down and run and keep on running, but I was determined to save the world, so I filled out a blue form that enabled me to go to another 2000 similar gatherings over the next quarter of a century.

There were, if my memory serves me correctly, another fifteen or so hardy souls present, whom I knew were alive because every now and then one of them would move. It was only a flicker, but it was enough to let me know that we were not at Madame Tussauds.

It was where I first got a full understanding of the word stoic, which is defined in the *Macquarie Dictionary* as, 'pertaining to the school of philosophy founded by Zeno, 475 BC, who taught that men should be free of passion, unmoved by joy or grief, and submit without complaint to unavoidable necessity'.

It is the pose adopted by the overwhelming majority of those who since 1891 at Barcaldine or Balmain have suffered the excruciating boredom of an Australian Labor Party branch meeting.

I checked the blue membership form I had signed, just to make sure I had not given them permission to perform a frontal lobotomy on me. Most of those present seemed to have had one, or alternatively, they were candidates for the George Cross. I was to learn later that in the dim distant past some personage of Socratic wisdom had moved and had passed at a State Conference that no branch meeting, no matter what the reason, could go on past two hours, plus one half-hour extension. If there is to be a heaven, that good soul should sit on the right hand of Himself.

No sooner had I joined or thought I had joined the Australian Labor Party, than I received another visit from 'Dentures'. This was to inform me that a new branch of the Party was to be formed at Asquith and that as I lived within the newly defined boundaries, would I kindly present myself at Hornsby Railway Station the following Tuesday night where a meeting would be held to 'discuss' this pioneering effort.

'Discuss' was the operative word. It was to be that moment of truth when you ask yourself the question 'Do I really want to save mankind, or should I join the Darts Club?' Hornsby Railway Station is not now a particularly good advertisement for a socialised transport system unless of course you've travelled on the New York subway. In 1964 it was even less prepossessing.

I found the room where the meeting was being held by simply assuming that either someone was being murdered or it was the ALP at play. The room was one of those that was so dark and dingy that when you turned the light on the room got darker.

Sitting in the room were four people, three of whom were hurling abuse at each other, while the fourth, my old mate 'Dentures', watched in silent resignation. My arrival increased the branch attendance by 25 per cent.

Chairing the meeting was a burly Yorkshireman with an accent you could cut with a knife. 'Bruvver Ducker', as he was affectionately known, was then a minor luminary in both the Party and the union movement, but was later to become State President and one of the Party's major Right-wing power brokers. To me he was just another Pom, although I must say, one I was quickly starting to feel sorry for. The two who were shouting at him were an elderly couple who were introduced to me as Jack and Agnes Healy. They stopped shouting at each other long enough to say hello and then resumed at full throttle.

With the light in my eyes of the convert who had decided to dedicate the rest of his life to social justice, eliminating poverty and bringing about world peace, I was, to say the least, a little shocked at my new found partners. I was also mesmerised by the language they spoke: Groupers, FECs, SECs, National Civic Council, Santamaria, Right-wingers, Left-wingers ... they may as well have been speaking in Hindustani. I watched fascinated as the combatants went at it hammer and tongs. I had to admit it was livelier than my first meeting, but not quite what I had expected. I was to learn that Labor Party branch meetings were usually like this — funereal or explosive. There was no in-between.

A month later I attended my third meeting, only this time it was at the local school and when, the following month, I attended my fourth meeting at Asquith shopping centre I gave them points for variety. Each new meeting-place I attended was a mile or so further north. It occurred to me that if I stayed in the Party long enough I would see the whole east coast of Australia.

Interestingly, I still was not officially a member of the ALP. The blue form I had filled out at my initial meeting-place had not followed me on my journey north. That was hardly surprising, I suppose. I was having difficulty following myself.

It was to be November before I finally got my ticket that showed that I was now a 'card-carrying member' of the great Australian Labor Party. I wondered how the less determined fared.

Now that I was a 'Party member' my elation knew no

bounds. When I announced to friends that I had joined I got quite a thrill out of the level of shock/horror or just stunned amazement that came over them. I felt, I imagined, like someone living in Europe during World War II who had just told his parents that he had joined the partisans.

It didn't take long for the sense of excitement to diminish. One only had to go to regular branch meetings to get the pulse rate down to about 30. My initial fervour was generated by the anticipated intellectual stimulation I would get at these 'cell' meetings when we would discuss our solutions to the problems that beset the world — Civil Rights battles in the United States, apartheid, Rhodesia, Vietnam and the plight of Australia's Aborigines. Ah, the sweet innocence of youth — if you can describe 29 as youthful.

The lovely Rae, who was I think, more than a little surprised at the fact that I had actually gone through with it and become a Party member, still treated my boyish enthusiasm with an air of patronising condescension.

'Solved any of the major world problems?' she would enquire, as I came home from the monthly meeting.

'Well, solved is probably not the word. We've started a little more modestly than I anticipated,' I informed her. 'We've settled for seeking solutions for the hole in the road outside the pub, the trees growing out over Linda Street and Mr Clough's suspension.'

My life in politics had begun.

THE LAST RIGHTS

Few people gave me more pleasure or more sound political advice than Fred Daly, MP for over thirty years, Minister in the Whitlam Government, humorist, Rugby League fan and one of the most popular political figures of the postwar period.

Elected to Parliament in 1943, he is one of the last links with many of the greats of the past — Lang, Scullin, Curtin, Chifley. Being one of the handful of MPs who has served over thirty years, at 74 he has outlived many of his contemporaries. After over fifty years in politics, he has attended many of their funerals.

On one occasion, Fred attended a funeral of one of the most disliked politicians in the Party. He was amazed at the extraordinarily large gathering of mourners around the grave. Turning to a colleague standing beside him, he commented about the size of the crowd and how surprised he was. 'They all hated him!' said Fred.

'Yes,' replied the colleague through gritted teeth, 'that's why they're here. To make sure he's buried!'

A FOND FAREWELL

Funerals are one of the great Labor rituals. The last in fact. It is one of the few aspects of living and dying that the Labor Party doesn't have a set of rules about. They do, however, attract large gatherings of the faithful to farewell those who have attended their last Caucus meeting. An occasional tear is shed, usually by the bereaved family, as the survivors mingle during breaks in the service, discussing the many virtues of the dear departed.

As Senator Pat Kennelly, one of the real characters of the postwar period, with the most famous stutter in politics, so aptly put it when describing a funeral of a colleague that he had recently attended: 'It was a very move ... move ... move ... moving occasion. They ... they ... they were g-g-g-gathered around the g-g-g-grave. Not a dry eye in sight. With but one ... one thought in mind. WHO ... WHO ... WHO ... WHO'S GOING TO WIN THE PRE-SELECTION?'

THE ONLY REQUIREMENT

State funerals are reserved for Ministers or above. They are solemn but quite impressive events, with lots of pomp and ceremony.

As a young politician, Fred attended his first State funeral and was suitably impressed. He turned to a senior MP beside him, in wonderment. 'Jeez, what do you have to be to get one of these?' he asked innocently.

The old pro looked down at him, touched by the innocence of youth, and replied solemnly, 'DEAD!'

AN INFREQUENT VISITOR

Fred was not one of Jack Lang's admirers. Having seen what Lang did to split the Party in the 1930s and listened to him bucket the Chifley Labor Government during a three-year stint in Federal Parliament from 1946-9, Fred bitterly opposed Lang's readmission to the Party, moved so eloquently by his friend, Paul Keating, at the New South Wales State Conference in 1971. Fred was unmoved by the fact that 'the Big Fella' was nearing the century mark.

When finally Lang died at the age of 97, he was given a State funeral at St Mary's Cathedral, attended by a huge crowd of mourners. The Requiem Mass was performed by the Archbishop, who spoke in glowing terms of Lang's contribution to the community. Fred, who was not among the mourners, bumped into His Grace shortly afterwards.

'Gawd, you must be getting desperate for bodies!' Fred told his co-religionist. 'That'd be Lang's second visit to church and both times he was carried in.'

SMILE, YOU'RE ON CANDID CAMERA!

After a disastrous family holiday on Dunk Island during the Christmas of 1970, when we had been buffeted between Cyclones Althea and Bronwyn, Rae and I decided that we should be a little mutinous, and we headed north-east for a vacation among the survivors of the *Bounty*. Word of our arrival had reached the ears of the President of the Norfolk Island branch of the Australian Labor Party, Ab Bathey, who was round to greet us on our arrival with the news that we were soon to be joined by Senator and Mrs McClelland. As old friends of Doug and Lorna, we were delighted that they were about to join us on our island sojourn. We decided to surprise them by being at the airport when they arrived.

It was Rae and I who were surprised as Senator Jim and Freda McClelland stepped off the plane. Jim had been elected in late 1970, but had taken his seat early, due to the untimely death of Senator Jim Ormonde. It was to be the beginning of a long friendship.

Jim was less than delighted to learn that we had been invited to an ALP function to meet the locals. It was not what he had in mind for his holiday. I agreed with him, but we went and enjoyed the company of a delightful group of people.

Among the guests, to my surprise, was a State MP, who had represented one of the inner working-class suburbs of Sydney for many years. A lovable Runyonesque character, he was one of those who were often referred to as 'the fruit barrow boys', a reference to the practice of handing out fruit barrow licences to friends of the Party. His tough upbringing had led him to a careless regard for the finer points of the law; he adopted a Robin Hood attitude for 'taking from the rich and giving to the poor'. He was, however, generous to a fault, so that whilst he defined his own economic status as decidedly poor, he always gave generously to any battler that needed a hand.

One aspect of the law with which he was totally unfamiliar was that concerning electoral matters. Rumour has it that the old adage 'vote early, vote often' if not said by him, had at least been adopted as the family motto. Some years earlier, during one Royal Commission into an election result, it had been alleged that, among many other claims of electoral fraud, his brother had voted thirty-two times! Both of them were tireless workers for the Party, particularly when armed with a pencil.

He had kindly offered to help me in my initial campaign in 1969, after telling me that he could not understand how Labor had lost the previous Sydney City Council elections.

'How'd they get beat with nineteen entrances to the polling booths?' he asked rhetorically, shaking his head more in sorrow than in anger. 'Yer can't get beat with nineteen entrances — it's impossible!'

I had gently rejected his offer, informing him that I wanted to win fairly and that I didn't want any allegations of electoral malpractice following me around afterward. I might have added, 'As they have you, for the past thirty years.'

He looked at me totally bewildered, unable to understand my thought processes. 'Better the candidate don't know, mate! Better the candidate don't know!' To the best of my knowledge, he stayed out of the campaign.

His own electorate was one of the seediest in Sydney and he was often criticised for the company he kept. 'Listen,' he would say, 'if I don't talk to pimps, pros and crooks, I'd talk to no one!'

Sticking to his principles, he had arrived on Norfolk with three characters who, one felt, may have rubbed shoulders with the seamier side of life. Two very blonde and buxom ladies and a 'gentleman' who we came to know as George. Hair brilliantined and parted in the middle, a double-breasted pin-striped suit, diamond stick pin, two-tone shoes and a heavy European accent made him appear as if he had stepped straight out of 'The Untouchables'.

The four of us had only just arrived when we were spotted by our State colleague. In a manner developed no doubt from years of exposure to his constituents, he sidled up to us and out of the corner of his mouth whispered conspiratorially, 'Be nice to George — great friend of the Party . . . great friend of the Party!' He motioned with a cupped right hand and a wink that implied that George regularly and generously 'tipped in'.

Over the next four days, whenever we came across each other, as we inevitably did on such a small island as Norfolk, we would be constantly reassured by our friend that 'George was a great friend of the Party!' I never doubted it.

Jim McClelland and his delightful wife, Freda, who died tragically some years later, were as unlike our colleague and his friends as any two people could be. Jim, handsome, elegant and one of the most articulate men I have ever met, was to become Minister for Manufacturing Industry, then Minister for Labour and Immigration in the Whitlam Government and later Chief Judge of the Land and Environment Court of New South Wales. An excellent dress sense and a taste for the finer things in life earned him the soubriquet 'Diamond Jim'.

Whenever we met up with George and Co., Jim's expression would range from one of amused disdain to that which one gets when passing the local dunny. I was therefore more than a little surprised when Jim agreed to George's continued blandishments to join his party for dinner.

I was equally surprised that the evening went remarkably smoothly, with Jim trying his hardest to develop the 'common touch'. It was not a role he found easy. However, as the evening wore on and some mild libation was had by all, the mood changed and I even suspect that Jim started to warm to the lovable rogue and his friends.

The ladies, obviously of independent means, were determined to show us all the 'goodies' they had bought on Norfolk Island. Freda and Rae were fascinated by the large cowrie shell with the flashing light. They had also managed to buy half the electronic equipment on Norfolk and a very expensive camera.

The evening reached its climax when suddenly one of the blondes leapt on to a chair, pointed her camera at Jim and shrieked, 'Smile!' With that, George and the other blonde put their arms around Jim, as the camera went 'pop!'.

'Diamond Jim' paled visibly and the last remaining hairs on his head went white. I could hear him audibly groan, 'Oh, no!' I knew what he was thinking. As we left the restaurant, he turned to me and whispered, "That photo will come back to haunt me. One day, when it really matters, I shall have that photograph shoved in front of me and be asked to explain about my "friend" George!'

Some weeks after our return, Jim phoned. 'I just thought you'd like to know, son, that George is the proprietor of the —— Club [one of Sydney's infamous baccarat clubs].'

LOST IN THE FOREST

One of my most endearing qualities is that I am a trusting soul. It is a quality rare among politicians, as anyone who knows the New South Wales Party machine will attest. My problem is that if people tell me somthing, I take them at face value until I have evidence to the contrary. So when our far-flung cousins the Western Australians invited me to undertake a tour of the south-western electorate of Forrest, I believed them when they said it would be leisurely and enjoyable.

It has become fashionable among political pundits to attribute Labor's success in the 1980s to the professionalism of its organisation. Labor's well-oiled machine is so far superior to its opponents' that it's a wonder they bother at all. That theory has come slightly unstuck in recent months, particularly since the New South Wales elections.

However, this was 1978, and I was enjoying with boyish enthusiasm my first stint on the front bench as Bill Hayden's Shadow Minister for Sport, Recreation, Tourism and The Environment, and, dare I say, its spokesman on Women's Affairs.

The electorate of Forrest in any other State or country would be considered an extremely large one. Taking up the south-west corner of Western Australia, it included then the towns of Bunbury, Busselton, Manjimup and Albany. Its sitting member at the time was the gentle and likeable Peter Drummond, representing the Liberal Party. Named after Lord Forrest, the famous explorer and MP at the time of Federation, it had been held by the Liberals at every election, excluding the freak result achieved in 1969, when the late Frank Kirwan held it briefly for three years.

It was not a seat one would have thought would be high on the Western Australian branch's list of priorities. Apparently, however the local branches in Forrest had been complaining quite bitterly that they never saw any Federal MPs, particularly Shadow Ministers, and they felt neglected. I was to find out why.

Wide-eyed and innocent, I arrived in Perth, jet-lagged by the 4,500-kilometre trip, to be met by the Secretary of the Western Australian branch, Gordon Hill, and 100-kilometre winds and rain. It was not a good start. There is a point in any journey when you know you should turn back, but you foolishly continue. I continued.

Our first call, I was informed by Gordon, was to inspect a drain which was leaking something nasty into a lake. I thought for a minute he was joking.

'Surely,' I asked, 'this is a local government matter, hardly warranting an inspection by a Federal Shadow Minister?'

'Well, it's very important to the local branch secretary,'

he informed me. 'She's been on about it for years.' It was that moment of enlightenment when all is fully revealed. I was on a 'search and massage' tour to cover up the area's neglect by the State branch.

Minutes later, I was standing beside a metre-wide drain, surrounded by ten bedraggled executives of a mineral processing company and the branch secretary, watching a tiny trickle of brown muck float gently into a lake the size of a small sea. It hardly looked like 'Love Canal'. I looked up at the executives, staring balefully down at the trickle, while the wind and rain swept and howled around their persons.

If it is possible for a socialist to feel desperately sorry for capitalists, this was that moment. I tried by facial twitches and body language to say as best I could, 'I'm sorry.' To this day I'm sure the poor wretches understood. I could detect a flutter of recognition and gratitude for my gesture of sympathy.

I glanced sideways at the drenched, homespun figure of the secretary. The expression on her face was positively orgasmic. A mixture of triumph and contempt swept over her visage as she glowed with delight at their discomfiture. As we drove off in Gordon's car towards our next appointment, I muttered something about 'there not being many more like that'. I was to be disappointed.

My itinerary had stated simply 1 pm: Address Bunbury Tourist Association? It had been my practice during my period as Shadow Minister, to prepare typed speeches of approximately fifteen pages for functions such as these. Usually a luncheon was held in a local restaurant or hotel for about thirty or so of the local tourist personnel — motel owners, tour operators and so forth. Having made the speech so often I had decided on this occasion that I would just use notes. It was probably the only perspicacious act on my part during the whole tour.

Arriving at my destination, I was met by a small, rotund gentleman I guessed to be in his mid-sixties. In his arms he held a small bundle of dripping hair that repeatedly barked and snapped at me 'Welcome to the 'Leschenault Lady'! He cried.

"I beg your pardon? I said.

"The *Leschenault Lady!*' he cried.

'I beg your pardon?' I said.

'The Leschenault Lady,' he repeated.

I was not sure quite what it was that he was offering me.

'It's a train,' he explained. Slowly the fog lifted and I started to understand what he was saying 'The *Leschenault Lady*' was a vintage train that was his pride and joy. It had, he explained, been faithfully restored courtesy of a grant from the Whitlam Government. He was inviting me to intimately inspect 'The Lady'. An offer, as they say, too good to refuse.

'What about the Bunbury Tourist Association?' I asked. 'I'm supposed to speak to them.'

'You are!'

'I beg your pardon?' I sounded like a cracked record.

'I'm the Bunbury Tourist Association!' he proclaimed proudly. I looked around for my guide, but he had quietly slipped away for lunch. All I wanted to do was to get my hands around his neck. For the next hour and a half, I was given a very wet and windy conducted tour of 'The Lady' by a man and his dog.

When my guide returned some time later, he announced, 'We should have had you at the "Fun Run". There were over five hundred people there.' I couldn't think of a suitable reply.

At this stage, Gordon, who I suspect anticipated what the rest of the week would be like, handed me over like a baton to the lady who was to accompany me on the rest of my tour. Still wringing wet and covered in diesel oil, I relaxed as my new chauffeur set forth on the next leg of our journey to the seaside village of Busselton, half an hour's drive from Bunbury.

Its sole, distinguishing feature is a jetty, known not surprisingly as the Busselton Jetty. It stretches across the Indian Ocean, halfway to South Africa.

I had learnt of this maritime wonder solely due to one Fred Bussell ringing me in Parliament House at all hours of the day and night to solicit my support in restoring this family monument. It appears that on a dark and stormy night, not dissimilar to the present clime we were enjoying, a stronger than normal gust of wind had cut a swathe throught the Busselton jetty, rendering it inoperative for the thousands upon thousands of enthusiastic anglers who I was assured depended upon it for their living and/or sport.

The future of Busselton, the fishermen, the Western Australian tourist industry and the peace of mind of Fred Bussell were all dependent upon the Federal Government providing a mere six million dollars required to return the Jetty to its former glory. It appears that successive Liberal Ministers had sympathised with, but done nothing about, Mr Bussell's modest request. It was beholden on any visiting VIP, even a Labor shadow minister, to make the obligatory visit to the famous jetty to inspect this international tragedy. I was no exception.

After making the appropriate noises expected of a witness to such a tragedy, we adjourned to the local council rooms to discuss with the good burghers of Busselton the best method of acquiring the piffling six million dollars (at 1978 prices). In my most obsequious manner, I assured them I would do everything in my power, make appropriate representations, etc. etc., to help them solve the problem. To the best of my knowledge, the Busselton Jetty has the same hang-dog look it had a decade ago. At least Fred Bussell no longer phones me late at night.

The itinerary informed us that we were then to break bread with the Party faithfuls at 4 pm. We arrived precisely at four and were greeted by a stream of branch members headed in the opposite direction.

'Yer too late, mate! You was supposed to be 'ere an hour ago!' growled one of the departing guests. We shared the crumbs of a sponge cake and a cold cuppa with our apologetic hosts.

The highlight of the first day's triumphant tour of the West was to be the inevitable travelling ALP barbecue that follows MPs around Australia. Whenever funds are needed, as they inevitably are, the cry goes out to the faithful, 'Let's have a barbecue!' Five dollars a head and the kids free usually results in the branch finances being further reduced, as everyone gorges themselves on char-burned steak and coleslaw. If it rains, as it inevitably does, you're up to your arsehole in coleslaw for a week. So it was that after a mad rush back to Bunbury to change into barbie clobber, we arrived at the joint Bunbury-Busselton ALP barbecue in honour of the visiting Shadow Minister for Sport, Recreation, Tourism and The Environment.

'We don't see many of youse Canberra blokes over here!' I was informed by a sturdy yeoman, swigging a tinnie, as I arrived. I looked at the three other guests who made up the full complement of those who had come to pay me homage.

'I wonder why?' I replied.

SPOOKS

Early in 1978, after Labor's second successive thrashing by Fraser at the polls, the story broke in the Murdoch Press that Whitlam, Federal Secretary of the ALP David Coombe and Victorian Left-winger Bill Hartley had been negotiating with agents of the Iraqi Baathist Party to obtain up to half a million dollars to help fund the 1977 election.

No one would have been surprised by the connections of the loopy Hartley, who seemed to delight in embarrassing the ALP with his involvement with every murderous fanatic in the Middle East, but Whitlam and Coombe's involvement turned the matter into a major embarrassment for the

Party. The headlines ran for days with the Murdoch Press leading the charge for Gough's sacking.

A special Federal Executive meeting was called for 4 and 5 March. A bizarre twist to the crisis the Party was wallowing in occurred as the erratic Hartley implied in public utterances that the then President of the Australian Labor Party, Bob Hawke, was in league with Israeli Intelligence and the CIA. Rumours abounded of plots and counter plots. The Left of the Labor Party are paranoid about ASIO and the CIA and go ape at the mention of Israelis. Having raised paranoia to an art form, they were at fever pitch when the Federal Executive met on the morning of 4 March. The meeting started in an atmosphere of distrust as conversation centred around spooks. Suddenly a loud buzzing noise rent the air! The already nervous delegates jumped out of their seats. Hartley leaped to his feet announcing that the room was bugged and proceeded to search for the offending device.

After some confusion the mild-mannered and partially deaf member of the Left-wing, Arthur Geitzelt, announced, 'I'm awfully sorry, it's my new hearing aid. I can't work it properly!'

GÖTTERDÄMMERUNG

Bob Hawke has had his share of bad weeks, but few to match the disastrous first weekend in February 1988. On Saturday 6 February, Labor lost the blue ribbon Labor seat of Adelaide, occasioned by the resignation of former Immigration Minister Chris Hurford. On the Sunday came the devastating announcement that Labor's most popular Minister, Mick Young, had resigned from both the Cabinet and the Parliament.

On the Wednesday I received the following invitation postmarked 8 February, from the member for Maribyrnong, Alan Griffiths.

Dear Barry,

March 5th is of course the fifth anniversary of the election of the Hawke Labor Government.

I thought this occasion should be celebrated in a way other than the usual dinner with speeches etc.

Accordingly, I have booked the magnificently restored Walter Burley Griffin INCINERATOR Theatre Complex for a much more relaxing and enjoyable get together . . .

GUESS WHO'S COMING TO DINNER?

When the Parliamentary Catering Service sent my monthly statement for July 1987, I was surprised that it showed I owed them $1.92. As entertainment as a Minister had usually left me with a monthly bill of around $300, it was not the size of the bill, but the fact that there was any bill at all. Having only spent one day in July in Canberra — the day of the ballot for the third Hawke Ministry — and recalling that my wife Rae and I had departed Canberra around midday, I was wondering how I had managed to spend even $1.92. Curious, I turned to the attached invoice, which read as follows:

SPLIT CHARGE TO:	HON. B. COHEN MP
DATE	21.7.87
LOCATION	SENATE #3
FUNCTION	PARTY MEETING
ORDERED BY	SEN. RICHARDSON
AMOUNT	$1.92

I think the expression is 'He gave a wry smile'. The account was for the supper served at the meeting called by the Centre Unity faction leader, Senator Graham Richardson, to determine who would be the Right-wing's Ministerial nominations. Well aware of the hatchet job that Graham had in store for me so that he could take over my ministerial portfolio of Arts, Heritage and Environment, I had decided that I would rather not attend. Graham must have imagined that I was there with him, at least in spirit.

Even Christ did not pay for the Last Supper!

> **Gordon Scholes — February 1971**
> Migrants arriving in Australia will not get a vote for five years after their arrival unless they are English migrants who usually can speak English.

THE FIRST LADY

LOST FOR WORDS

We had been married less than a week. Our elopement had meant that we had missed out on all the wedding goodies that a young couple uses to furnish the rented garret.

Rae's glory box, containing teatowels and sheets, ensured that we ate with clean knives and forks and didn't suffer from skin rash. The grotty half of a Federation duplex, in which my mad former Science Master nightly brawled with his partner of four or five decades, had been rented for two weeks in advance with 16 pounds borrowed from my father. Apart from a toaster and some cups and saucers as wedding gifts, we had it all in front of us.

It was, as I recall, our fourth post-nuptial evening together when I arrived home from work worried about where the next fortnight's rent was coming from. There had been no honeymoon. We were far too poor for that.

The bride, in all her loveliness, was sitting in the dark and dingy dining-room caressing a book. Not an ordinary book, mark you, but the largest I had ever seen. It stood, in its fawn hard cover, almost a foot, not in height, but in depth. Her face was wreathed with a childlike smile. When Rae smiled, she could brighten even our dining dungeon.

'What's that?' I asked.

'A book.'

'I can see that, but what sort of book?'

She was still smiling angelically, as if in a trance.

'A WEBSTER'S DICTIONARY.' She spoke the words breathlessly, as if she were telling me we had just inherited the Koh-i-noor Diamond.

'Oh!' I could think of little else to say. 'Where did you get it?' I asked, being unable to recall her mentioning it before.

'I've always, always wanted a *Webster's Dictionary*!' She continued ignoring my question, while gently caressing its cover in a way every man would like to be touched. 'I bought it today from a travelling salesman. Ten pounds, two shillings a week. Isn't it wonderful?'

There are moments like these in every man's life. I looked around at our humble abode. I recalled the agony of finding next week's rent. I thought of all the things we needed for our future together. I tried desperately to find words to express my feelings. Nothing I could think of could do justice to this moment. I knew then why I had married her.

FARMER RAE

> Ours is a nice 'ouse ours is
> It's got no rats or mouses.

No, but it's got or has had almost every other type of bloody animal that lives or breathes. Let's face it, I married an animal nutter. Maybe because of my long absences from home animals became a substitute. Whatever the reason Rae has put together a fair collection for a family that aren't actually farmers. At present the following share EMOH RUO at Matcham Road, Matcham with the Cohen family:

- Yoni — donkey (male)
- Sheba — Shetland pony (female)
- Ali — goat (male)
- Rocky — wallaroo (male)
- Cassie — wallaroo (female)
- Toddy — Shetland sheep dog (male)
- Whisky — Shetland sheep dog (female)
- Simba — cat (male)
- Nelson — cat (male)

To coin a phrase, 'You don't have to be mad to live in our house but it helps.' I say this because precisely at the time of writing — 1.30 am, 5 January 1988 — Simba, the cat, is scratching at the front door demanding to be let out at the same time as Rocky, the wallaroo, is scratching at the rear window demanding to be let in.

Rae finds nothing particularly strange in this, but she finds nothing particularly strange in the behaviour of any of our 'family'.

'Simba!' she cries to the senior feline member of the family, 'you can't get out the front door because it's locked.' Rae is bilingual. She speaks English and Cat. Unfortunately, Simba doesn't and continues to scratch at the door until the resident idiot, the local Federal Member, gets up and opens it. Simba, who has been accompanying his scratching with appropriate wailing, acknowledges this act of kindness by stalking past without so much as a by-your-leave as he wanders out into the night to terrorise the local inhabitants.

Rarely a night passes without Simba, 'the killer cat', presenting us with his evening catch. At some time, usually between midnight and dawn, we are awakened by a wail that sounds like 'hello' from the lounge-room. It is repeated at regular intervals until one of us, usually yours truly, arises to examine the 'kill' and congratulate the killer so that we can all get some sleep. I usually award him both ears and the tail.

Anyone who wonders why some of the smallest of Australia's indigenous species are endangered need only examine the smorgasbord of partly chewed birds, possums, bandicoots and gliders whose remains are splattered across our blood-stained lounge-room carpet. I don't mind the rats, mice and rabbits being part of the menu, but I have to wrestle with my conscience about some of the other species as a former Environment Minister, not to mention the durability of my marriage to my feline-loving wife. I've never been courageous enough to issue the challenge 'Simba or ME!'

Simba and his nocturnal maraudings are merely the latest chapter in the feathered and furry capers that have marked our near thirty-year union. I married the dear girl blissfully unaware that she was mentally unstable. Of course I was aware that, like any normal child, she had possessed a couple of dogs with whom she had formed a close, even loving relationship. During our courtship it was beholden on me to listen with rapt attention to the magnificent adventures of the two cocker spaniels, Prince and Monty, who had shared her affection prior to my arrival on the scene. As a naive, unsuspecting, some would say besotted suitor, I was hardly in the position to make an objective assessment of her state of mind. A passionate love affair with two canines seemed to me to be a not unhealthy state of mind for a young gel. The signs were there but, to coin a phrase, 'Love is blind' and so was I. The disease she suffers from I believe is known as canine dementia.

I guess I was lulled into a false sense of security when she told me how much she hated cats. We can all be grateful for that. After Kenzi, Maynard, Casper, Snoopy, Peanuts, Winkie, Crud, Nelson and Simba, one wonders what life would have been like had she actually liked cats.

We had only started to share our life together when Rae became pregnant with Stuart and Jasper. Stuart arrived hairless, Jasper, a Pembrokeshire corgi, a ball of piddling fur. He was the first of a long line of uncontrolled bladders that have cost me a fortune in carpets. Ticks and cars are among the deadly hazards that prey upon four-legged friends and so it was that Jasper and his successor departed for the Big Kennel in the sky.

The first to live to healthy middle-age was a Cardiganshire corgi affectionately known as — Gough. I was never quite sure whether the other one took it as a compliment or an insult. He just used to give me a peculiar look whenever I mentioned our dog by name.

It was nothing, however, compared with the expression on Lionel Murphy's face when he and Ingrid were guests at a dinner party at our Turramurra home and I ordered

'Gough' to stop sniffing round the guests' feet.

'I thought Gough was going to piss on your foot,' I informed the startled Senator, forgetting for the moment that he was unaware of precisely whom I was referring to.

When we found an abandoned kitten during a return visit from Gosford the opportunity presented itself to complete the pair and the new member of the family was duly named Margaret. It was some days later when closer examination forced us to change 'her' name to Maynard.

Providing names for an endless stream of pets taxes the imagination of the less creative among us, but not No 2 son Martin, who has provided handles for a succession of birds: Zongo Zapfield III to Ziffel and Eek. The last earned her soubriquet from her limited vocabulary. Fruitcake, the rabbit, earned his name from the raisins he deposited on the carpet.

I wouldn't want people to think that because of my wife's part bog-Irish ancestry all the animals were allowed into the house. We've had dogs, cats, budgies, rabbits, goats, kangaroos as well as horses, a pony and a donkey. Let me assure you that none of the last group has been in the house. That's not to say she didn't suggest it. Shortly after the acquisition of Rocky and Cassie, we were frequently awakened by the shrieks of house guests who awoke to find two wallaroos hopping around their bedroom.

The first decade of our union was marked by the conventional acquisition of traditional pets: dogs, cats and birds. After my election to Parliament in 1969 and our subsequent move to a 5 acre farm at Matcham, there was a distinct policy shift. It all started one afternoon when the little woman opined that it was about time we put the four unused acres to appropriate commercial use.

'I could buy some calves, fatten them up and sell them at a handsome profit!'

It occurred to me that my socialist colleagues might not take too kindly to my playing the country squire. Still, the idea of putting the land to good use, keeping the grass down and Rae occupied, had a certain appeal. Any lingering doubts were dispelled when, with Rae's birthday fast approaching, I heard of a calf on offer for 15 dollars.

I must confess to feeling rather smug seeing the look of ecstasy on her face as I presented her with a black and white birthday present. I had made my wife very happy, acquired a lawn mower, fertiliser and a sound investment, all for 15 dollars. How shrewd can you get?

Just how shrewd was driven home to me a few days later when she mentioned casually that of course we'd have to get a fence to keep Jeremiah in. No animal had been more aptly named. And then of course there was the vet. Jeremiah was a bottomless pit. When he wasn't visiting his doctor he was eating, and not just what grew on the property. Suddenly this black and white chip investment had to have all sorts of supplementary feeds.

'We'll all be rooned,' I cried as I realised the name Cohen was to be added to the long list of Australian farming failures.

It was about this time that I also discovered something that gave me cause for grave disquiet about the 'good lady wife'. In her acquisition of four-legged friends she had a distinct preference for the male of the species, leading to a situation where, with our three sons, she was often the only female in residence.

She seemed to prefer them with less than their full manhood. All sorts of spurious reasons were given as to why they had to be cut, gelded, deknackered or whatever word was chosen to describe the most hideous of all crimes. Whatever it's called, the result was always the same. If any of them started to play up and cause trouble it was a quick call to Master Bates and snip snip . . . ugh . . . it really gets you where you live.

I must say though, it seemed to have the desired effect, not only on the four-legged animals. For at least a few weeks after the latest victim had been taken off in the tumbril, Stuart, Martin, Adam and I treated the First Lady of Matcham with the utmost respect. It probably explains why the Cohen men often appear to walk like Groucho Marx.

In fairness to Jeremiah, the thousand dollars or more spent on fencing, vets fees and feed appeared to be paying off. I watched our investment fatten to the point where on a dark night I often mistook him for my car. On a number of occasions I tentatively suggested that it was about time we cashed in Jeremiah, pointing out to my beloved that her original proposal to earn some money out of our acres had included a proposal to actually sell the fatted calf. I wondered whether Rae expected the abattoirs to pay us for baby-sitting Jeremiah. Such vulgar commercial suggestions were always greeted with the same outraged cry of 'Wash your mouth out' or a flood of tears. For days afterwards Rae would spend hours in the paddock with her arms around Jeremiah's beefy hide assuring him that I was only joking and/or a beast. I swear I saw Jeremiah alternately sniff and smirk at me as if to say, 'I'll outlive you sport.' The word went round among local cattle that the place to head for was Cohen's.

Just as I felt that Rae had finally succumbed to my blandishments to turn her prized steer into prime rump steak, lo and behold the lovely Jeremiah swallowed a bad ice cube and carked it. It was his last act of vengeance against me. Just when the abattoirs had made a tentative offer of 400 dollars, bye bye Jeremiah and surprise, surprise, a hundred dollars to have him buried.

Rae was in no way deterred by our attempt at ranching although our next try was slightly less ambitious. Profit-making was excluded from the Cohen lexicon and the more modest-sounding 'self-sufficiency' replaced it. Once again I was convinced by Rae's brilliant logic that the purchase of a rooster and some hens would guarantee us an unlimited supply of eggs which we would in turn barter for goods à la 'The Good Life'. (Rugby League fans will have no difficulty in understanding how our Plymouth Rock rooster acquired his distinguished name of Arthur.) In theory it sounded foolproof. Arthur would be let loose among the hens and 'Voila! — eggs. They in turn would become chickens, chickens would become hens and in no time we would have an unlimited supply of free-range eggs and fresh barbecued chickens. It all sounded so simple.

Arthur performed up to expectations, and before long we had reached our legal limit of nineteen hens. (This was the maximum number permitted under State legislation for an unlicensed egg producer). I often wanted to meet the bureaucrat who struck on the magic figure of nineteen.

Eggs came in plentiful supply. In fact it was only after our egg mountain started to match the European wine lake that we suddenly realised that we were not a major egg-consuming family. Rae is an excellent cook, bordering on brilliant in fact, but she does not include breakfast among her areas of expertise. Basically, breakfast at the Cohen household is 'catch and kill your own'. Early on in our marriage Rae announced, 'If you want a hot breakfast, I'll set fire to your cornflakes.' Our three sons learnt to forage for themselves or go to school hungry. Cooking eggs was beyond them.

The monthly surplus did not in any way faze the First Lady. Libby and Monica, who worked with Rae in our fashion business at St Ives, suddenly found themselves being offered free-range eggs at a dollar per dozen, about one third of the retail price. Not surprisingly, they found the offer too good to refuse. Each week the family income was supplemented by as much as 5 dollars. We were in clover, which was more than I could say for the hens.

Our property at Matcham consisted of 5 acres of rich lush

pasture and one small strip of concrete pathway that leads to the garage. It was the route I took barefoot each morning to collect the papers. It still remains a mystery to me as to why our chooks insisted on crapping on the tiny strip of concrete. It was equally mystifying that I rarely ever remembered their chosen site to empty their bowels. Each morning I would stagger up the path for the papers only to feel the warm soft sticky stuff squeeze gently up between my toes. It was not a good way to start the day.

I must say in fairness to our feathered friends they did not restrict their crapping solely to the footpath. As 'free rangers' they decided to make their home in the garage with the result that Rae's and my car normally looked like a pair of mating leopards. In time our house had both the look and the odour of a country outhouse. It was rumoured that behind our backs we were referred to by the locals as 'Ma and Pa Cohen'.

Ultimately, all good things come to an end. I told Rae she had to choose. There wasn't room for all of us at Matcham. A week later I got my answer. I could stay. An act of God helped her make the decision. Our poultry had contracted cancer and had to be put down. I reminded her that 'put down' was a euphemism for murder. Since the fiasco of the chooks, to her credit the Good Lady has not once suggested any further rural business ventures.

With chooks and cattle out of the way Rae's mind turned to goats. The excuse this time was to keep the grass down, and whilst not making a profit it was at least saving on slashers and gardeners. Our dreams of making our fortune had faded to self-sufficiency and finally to repairs and maintenance. We had certainly lowered our sights.

Had unexpected visitors turned up the night that Mandy and Randy arrived, the sight that greeted them may well have turned out to be just too much. Let loose in the backyard on a freezing cold winter's night, the goats had both promptly fallen in the pool:

Scene I — Mad woman dressed in full-length diaphanous nightgown, running up and down the swimming pool, shouts, "COME ON, Stuart! COME ON, Stuart!' as teenage boy swims the race of his life to defeat two goats in Matcham Cup.

Scene II — (fifteen minutes later). An even madder father of the house sits in front of TV, towelling shivering goats as they and the family watch 'Disneyland'.

A somewhat similar scene was to be replayed years later, when, as the Minister for the Environment, I suddenly acquired two baby wallaroos out of the blue from the Charleville district, courtesy of the late Phil Capewell. Just as I was about to step into my Commonwealth car before departing for Kingsford Smith Airport I heard a splash. Rushing to the fence I looked over to see the female of the species, by now affectionately known as Cassie, attempting the kangaroo crawl while her boyfriend, Rocky, looked on unmoved.

With a shriek, I took off. 'Raaaeee,' I screamed as I tore through the house shedding coat, trousers and shoes, on my frantic path down to the pool. Within second, I had dived in clad only in shirt, tie, underpants and socks and qualified for the animal version of the George Cross.

I often wondered how much the media would have paid for the picture of 'the Minister', wading triumphantly ashore clutching the hapless and shivering Cassie, as the Good Lady Rae and my driver Kerry Ternen stood on the top lawn, clutching their sides with tears streaming down their faces.

There are a million stories in the Naked City, and so it has been 'down on the farm'. During more than a quarter of a century of marriage, a fair number of furry and feathered friends have shared our lives. There has been tragedy and sadness, joy, love and loyalty. It has often been tumultuous but, thanks to Rae, never dull. As a socialist I have often felt guilty that we have spent enough money on our friends to have kept a Third World country in luxury, but I suspect that if I had the opportunity I'd do it all over again. However, I am grateful for many things, particularly that we live in Australia. You see, Rae's greatest love is ELEPHANTS!!

RAE-RAE IN CHINA

Whilst I wasn't surprised by how quickly the trappings of office disappeared when I became a 'Feather Duster', I was stunned by how quickly I was forgotten. After being a Director of the Australian Bicentennial Authority since its inception in 1980, the Minister responsible for the Bicentennial in the first Hawke Ministry and the Minister assisting the Prime Minister in the second, I was more than a little disappointed when I did not receive one invitation to any Bicentennial function apart from the one every member of parliament received for Australia Day. The National Institute of Dramatic Art (NIDA) soon forgot how hard I had fought to get them their new building.

I had become philosophical about the invitations I wasn't receiving until the pandas arrived in Australia. Despite some other people claiming to have thought of the idea, the plan to get the pandas was hatched in my office just prior to my cultural exchange visit to China in 1984. During the visit, in which I met with my opposite number in both the Environment and the Arts, I suggested to the Chinese officials that the Bicentennial gift that would be most appreciated by Australians would be pandas.

Rae and I visited the Wolong Panda Reserve in the mountains of China, near Tibet, where we had the opportunity to observe at first hand the magnificent research being undertaken jointly by the World Wildlife Fund and the Chinese Government to help ensure the survival of the

800-odd surviving pandas. Rae experienced the rare thrill of being present at the successful artificial insemination of Chin-Chin. I suggested to the Chinese that the offspring be called 'Rae-Rae'. On her return, Rae was invited by the former Ambassador to China, Hugh Dunn, to join a special committee to raise funds for the pandas' visit.

When a year or so later the Chinese announced that the pandas were coming to Australia for six months, we were very proud of the role we had played. I suppose we should not have been surprised when a certain national figure claimed it as all his own work. Still, as they say, that's politics. Nevertheless, I thought someone might have thought of inviting us to the welcoming party when the pandas arrived in March of 88.

The trip to China went very smoothly, except for one experience that taught me something new about the profession of journalism, Australian-style.

Arriving in Beijing after a long flight from Tokyo and a gruelling couple of days of official functions, Rae and I met the Australian press contingent based in the Capital. Official reception rooms in China all seem to be big enough for indoor tennis. Whilst I was doing an interview with a Chinese-Australian journalist from the ABC, Rae, exhausted from the tour so far, went to the other end of the 'ballroom', some 70 or 80 feet away and had a catnap.

After the interview, I was asked by the young lady if I would use my influence with the Chinese officials to obtain permission for her to visit the Wolong Panda Reserve to do a TV piece for ABC News. Up until then all her attempts had been unsuccessful. Throughout the rest of our tour, I constantly mentioned how important it was for Chinese-Australian relations for the young lady to be able to visit Wolong to let Australians know of the excellent work they were doing. As a result of my representations she arrived there a week or so after us. Imagine our surprise when we returned to Australia to be informed by friends that the only news that had come out of China about our trip was a report from a certain ABC reporter that, 'MRS COHEN, THE MINISTER'S WIFE, SLEPT THOUGH ALL HER HUSBAND'S SPEECHES'.

THE GREAT ESCAPE

The only resemblance between my brother Paul and me is that we both bear the name Cohen and, in our youth, had red hair. A Senior Lecturer in Anthropology at Macquarie University with a PhD, he is, as the 'Great Man' himself once described him, 'the cerebral one in the family'. We are all immensely proud of his academic achievements and my only envy of him is his sylph-like figure. Married to a delightful Thai lady, Julai, he has three children: Donna Lee, Angelique and Aree.

It has been our custom when travelling overseas to invite friends or relatives to stay at our home in Matcham to ensure that the place is looked after and also to ensure that the herd of animals is fed and watered.

Just prior to one overseas trip with the whole family, we had permitted our two corgis, Gus and Sally, to play 'mothers and fathers' at least once before they were put to the 'sword'. Corgis are usually an extremely neat and tidy breed of dog but like so many of our ventures into animal husbandry, this meeting was not a stunning success. The result was a litter of scraggy young scrubbers who, despite their lack of good breeding, were found homes where they were loved for their character rather than their looks. Our near neighbours, the Pearsalls, had been kind enough to take the ugliest of the bunch, one Taffy, who looked remarkably like a mop that had lost its handle.

Strict instructions had been left with Paul that the animals were not to be let out of the front door, nor was the side gate to be left open under any circumstances. He was warned that such a slip up would find him spending the rest of the day rounding up stray corgis.

Early one morning, just as the sun was rising, Paul was awakened by the melodic sounds of four corgis belting up and down Matcham Road, accompanied by the squeal of car tyres and the abuse of passing motorists.

Used to the leisurely life of the academic, the good doctor was not well prepared for rounding up herds of rampaging corgis at six in the morning. Always a lad with a strong sense of responsibility and one who quailed at the thought of facing the First Lady should one of her 'children' come to grief, he set off in spirited pursuit of the errant canines. It was, as they say, a hopeless task. Dogs know when they are out. To escape on their own to a forbidden area is a thrill known only to those who have led an imprisoned life. A mass break-out, as occurred on this fair day, was the sublime experience. No matter what inducement, promises, or threats of violence Paul offered, the magnificent four were not going to be coaxed back to 'Pentridge'.

Although Paul's specialist discipline is 'Onion farming in Thailand' something in the dim dark recesses of his mind, going back to his childhood when he too had owned pets, told him that only a massive bribe was going to solve the problem. Dashing to the refrigerator he extracted four prime lamb chops and took off once again in hot pursuit of the four escapees.

Local residents still talk of that morning and the sight that befell them as they drove to work and passed the local Member's residence. Clad only in striped pyjamas, a mad professor was seen running up and down Matcham Road, waving four lamb chops in the air whilst yelling terms of endearment at four equally frenzied corgis. It was not a pretty sight.

AND THEN THERE WERE FIVE

The day, however, was not yet over. Eventually our intrepid caretaker bribed the miscreants back into the corral. Bloodied but unbowed by his early morning cavortings, Paul relaxed with a good book, vowing that he would not show his face, or anything else that had been seen due to gaping pyjamas, during the rest of his holiday.

Unfortunately it had not occurred to Rae or me to inform my dear brother of the near daily practice of Taffy to come a-calling. That she had chosen this particular day above all others to make a visit was an act of canine sadism unknown hereabouts.

Paul had only just recovered from his earlier ordeal when he made the mistake of going outside to get some fresh air. Seconds later the bewildered lad raced back into the house and enquired of his wife, 'How many dogs have Rae and Barry got?'

'Four,' replied Julai.

'Are you sure?' asked Paul.

'Of course I'm sure,' came the reply.

'Are you sure? You're sure?' insisted Paul.

By now the normally patient Julai was becoming agitated by this fool of a man she had married. 'What do you mean? Are you mad? I'm feeding four dogs every day! You think I can't count?'

'No, no, my dear!' replied Paul, attempting to calm her without sounding patronising. 'This may come as a shock to you but there are now five corgis out in the backyard.

Julai was by now convinced that her husband had been sitting out in the sun for too long. A quick visit to the backyard convinced her otherwise.

'I'm sure there were only four!' she cried.

Paul was pensive for a moment, then in a manner not un-known among academics he announced, 'We have a visitor!'

'Well, we'll just have to get rid of him.' Julai smiled

sweetly, confident that the solution was at hand.

'There is only one problem,' posited the puzzled intellectual.

'What's that?'

'Which bloody one do I throw over the fence?'

DOUBLE VISION

Rae and I had arrived at the Ansett terminal to meet our close friend Mary Travers, of Peter, Paul and Mary fame, who was on her way from Melbourne after the conclusion of the group's stunningly successful 1967 tour of Australia.

'Who does that chap sitting over there remind you of?' I whispered to Rae, pointing to a balding, middle-aged gentleman with a beard, sitting alone about 20 feet from us and reading a book.

'Your father?'

'No, don't be silly, I'm serious. He's the dead spit of someone you've seen in films many times.'

'I don't know,' she sighed in that exasperated and patronising tone that wives reserve for husbands.

'Jose Ferrer!' I whispered.

'Who?'

'Jose Ferrer!!'

'Don't be ridiculous. He doesn't look anything like him.'

'But he does. He could be his double. It's extraordinary!' I was absolutely amazed by the likeness.

'Nonsense! You ought to get your eyes tested. Jose Ferrer, indeed!' she sniggered again as my temperature started to rise at the mocking tone in her voice.

'You're getting right up my nose,' I thought as I sat there simmering at Miss Smarty-pants.

A few minutes later a swarm of journalists and TV crews came galloping across the terminal shouting, 'Mr Ferrer, Mr Ferrer, can we get a few words . . .?'

THE ACE OF SPADES

'We've got some friends coming to dinner next week, if that's all right with you?' I announced to Rae, as I arrived one evening from the afternoon's practice at Tom Linsky's driving range.

'Oh! Who?'

'Tom and Susie Linsky, Terry and Kath Fowler and Lionel Martin.'

'Who,' she asked casually, 'is Lionel Martin?'

'A friend of Tom's,' I replied. 'He's a South African.'

There was a short silence before she answered. The tone was decidedly icy. 'A South African?'

'Yes.'

'A South African?'

But I thought I should bring this fairly limited conversation to an end. 'Do you have any objection to South Africans?' I asked as casually as I could.

Rae has the habit of coming straight to the point on occasions. 'You know I do! I don't want any bloody Nazis in my house!' she exploded.

'Now, my dear,' I said in my most patronising manner. 'You can't assume that because a person is a South African that they are all members of the Herstigte National Party.' (The extreme Right wing of the pro-Apartheid movement in South Africa.)

'I know what they're like,' she snarled. 'There aren't too many of them that don't hate the Blacks and you know what I'm like. We'll finish up having a brawl.'

I was well aware of what the good lady was like. Prior to our visit to South Africa in 1979, she deliberately went out and had an afro haircut and lay in the sun for a week so she could get up the noses of the whites.

'I don't understand you,' she said, knowing that I had led the opposition in Parliament to the Springbok Tour in 1971.

'Surely you checked out his views before you invited him home.'

'Well,' I said, retaining my composure in the face of this violent attack from my irate spouse, "I believe everyone is entitled to the benefit of the doubt. Maybe he's opposed to Apartheid.'

She muttered and grumbled for the rest of the week, but accepted the inevitable. Even she realised that I could hardly withdraw the invitation. She prepared for the dinner party with decidedly bad grace.

'This'll be a good night!' she announced, just before the guests were due to arrive. 'When we're not talking about golf, we'll be fighting about South Africa!'

The Linskys and Fowlers arrived promptly at eight, followed a few minutes later by Lionel. My only regret is that I didn't have a camera to capture for posterity the expression on the bride's face as his black visage appeared at the doorway.

'YOU . . .!!' she hissed at me.

ALL I WANT FOR CHRISTMAS

It comes as quite a shock to some Christians to learn that Jews do not celebrate Christmas. It would come as an even greater shock if they passed our farm in Matcham during the festive season. Out in the paddock is a Christmas tree. Nothing unusual about that I hear you say. True but not many Christmas trees have biscuits of hay, giant-sized bags of popcorn, tins of liver and turkey all neatly tied up with red and green bows with cards that read 'Merry Christmas Simba' or 'Happy Yuletide Yoni'— 'Love Mummy'.

The First Lady of Matcham regards Christmas as a very serious business and one that takes many weeks of planning. Whether you have two legs or four you receive a Christmas present. Last Christmas was no exception. Apart from the hay for Yoni and Sheba and the liver and turkey for Nelson and Simba there was a range of goodies for the rest. Nelson doubled up with a wind-up mouse and a placemat with printed instructions on it to 'HAVE A MICE MEAL'. Toddy, the elder of the Shetland sheepdogs, also scored a placemat for his saucer, although his had the instructions 'BONE APPETIT'. Ali, our permanent lawn-mower, got the giant plastic bag full of popcorn. Only a fence and a chain has stopped him from eating our house so we were not surprised when he attacked the popcorn with great gusto. A few hours later the vet had to be called to administer pills for a bad case of wind. Apparently goats and popcorn don't mix. Certainly not in the quantities Ali ate them. Despite his discomfort and the farting, he was able to relax under the new red, white and blue beach umbrella which he received every year. Rae thought it was a nice Bicentennial touch for a true blue Australian goat.

One year Ali received a beach towel and sunglasses, which he promptly ate. Passers-by shake their heads in disbelief even though it's been going on for years. Toddy and Whisky both got new sleeping baskets, Whisky because it was her first Christmas and Toddy because Whisky had eaten Toddy's basket.

They still talk in hushed tones about the horse's fly veil Rae bought for our late bull, the lovely Jeremiah, who had been seriously irritated during a particularly bad fly season. Unfortunately, bulls do not wear halters so the First Lady with her extraordinary capacity for innovation attached the veil to Jeremiah's horns. Jeremiah, it appeared, was not appreciative of her attempt to ease his discomfort and apparently found the veil more of an irritation than the flies. With a disdainful flick of his head Jeremiah converted the fly veil into a blonde wig, much to the astonishment of the local rustics.

DINNER WITH AUNTY

Like 'Quantum' and 'The Investigators', 'State of the Arts' was one of those innovative specialty programs that the ABC does so well. Regrettably, during one of its periodic scrambles after ratings the ABC decided to axe the first and only TV program that catered specifically for the arts during prime time.

During the period it was in full flight I was contacted by the program's excellent presenter, Andrew Saw, wanting to know if they could do a personal profile on me. I thought it over for thirty seconds and reluctantly agreed. Andrew explained that he wanted to capture me at home 'on the farm' in all my cultural glory.

Could I, he asked, invite a few of my 'intellectual' friends to partake of a Sunday luncheon in the garden room so that he could capture the scintillating conversation that they anticipated would ensue.

Knowing that anyone who was not invited would be grievously offended, the production was kept a deep dark secret that would have been the envy of the CIA.

John Wheeldon, the Whitlam Minister and now Associate Editor of the *Australian*, together with his headmistress wife Judy, were joined by Gary Simpson, university lecturer in education and the then Chairman of the Theatre Board of the Australia Council with his clinical psychologist wife Joan. We had thought of inviting Gore Vidal and Oscar Wilde but both were difficult to contact.

The garden room setting was fully wired for sound to the point where one became fearful of munching too enthusiastically on a chicken leg for fear of swallowing a microphone. The luncheon conversation was suitably brilliant and witty, if slightly stilted due to everyone being so conscious that every word, nuance or aside was being recorded for posterity to be broadcast nationwide.

The First Lady had gone to no end of trouble to ensure

the garden room was at its sparkling best, and the food would have done justice to Robert Carrier. Nothing was left to chance. The world would soon know that Matcham was about to rival Venice and Spoleto as a centre of artistic and intellectual excellence. Fifty years from now people would be famous for just having supped with the Cohens.

All our friends were given suitable advance notice as to when the 'State of the Arts' Cohen profile would be screened. Finally the big night arrived and we all sat in breathless anticipation, convinced that we were Logie material.

After much head and shoulders chat between Andrew and me we waited excitedly for the cameras to bring to the Nation the garden room, Rae's superb lunch, the Wheeldons, the Simpsons and the brilliant and witty conversation.

As the sun sank slowly in the west and the credits started to roll the cameras panned languidly across the farm to settle on Andrew's choice of the most intelligent contribution to the program — Yoni, our donkey.

IF MUZAK BE THE FOOD OF LIFE... I'LL STARVE TO DEATH!

One of Spike Milligan's passionate hatreds is muzak. A talented trumpet player who started his theatrical career in a jazz band, he despises its saccharine quality and its intrusive nature. He will often check with a restaurant before making a reservation to ensure he will not be driven mad by the infernal muzak.

On phoning his bank manager at Woy Woy one day and being asked to hold on for a while, he found himself listening to a particularly nauseating rendition of 'Greensleeves'. Eventually the manager came on the line. 'Yes, Mr Milligan, can I help you?'

Spike sang him 'The Desert Song' from go to whoa!

This story has absolutely nothing to do with Rae, except that she adores Spike and anyhow, I couldn't find any other chapter for it to go in!

IN THE SHOP

MADE TO MEASURE

If anyone sought my advice about going into clothing retailing, my answer would be very brief — 'DON'T!' I know of no better way of ageing prematurely unless you count politics. Many people mistake me for a 53-year-old when of course I am only 39!

During the 1960's, when I was sole proprietor of my men's wear store at St Ives, I decided that our fortunes would rise dramatically if I added suits to the range of clothing. The day of the bespoke tailor had long gone as the fractional fit suit replaced it.

The problem with 'ready mades' is that very few people are standard fittings. The infinite variety of shapes that the human body can come in is mind-boggling, as those who have seen me 'starkers' will testify. In attempting to cater for the many permutations and combinations that the flesh is heir to, a number of companies, Anthony Squires among them, decided to have a suit fitting for almost every imaginable slob. Where initially shops carried the standard 36, 38, 40, 42, 44-inch regular and similar sizes in short and long, resulting in about twelve basic fittings, they suddenly found themselves being offered up to 450 fractional fittings.

Fortunately this temporary insanity lasted for only a brief period. Unfortunately, I landed myself with some very odd-shaped suits, including one whose label bore the inscription, '40 SHORT PORTLY'. In the days when my figure was, well not beautiful, but believable, I wondered just precisely what a '40 SHORT PORTLY' looked like.

By an extraordinary coincidence I did not have long to wait. A rotund little fellow purchased the suit with the instructions that the trousers had to be lengthened 3 inches. When he returned the following day to try on the altered trousers, I heard an audible groan from the fitting-room. Rushing inside I was horrified to see that the pants had not only not been lengthened, they had been SHORTENED by 3 inches! With lots of bluster and quick action I had the pants off and the customer on his way with the assurance that the matter would be rectified on the morrow. Somehow or other the tailor who did the alterations was going to have to find 6 inches of material. I dared not look to see if there was that much to spare. I simply wrapped them up and wrote 'Lengthen 6 inches' on the parcel.

The day dawned with nary a hint of the events that would follow. The trusting soul arrived still smiling and innocently confident of the skills of the artisan and asked to try on his suit. He disappeared into the fitting-room. A few minutes later, whilst serving another customer, I noticed that my friend, whom I was getting to know quite well by now, had still not reappeared. The minutes ticked by and still no sign. A strange quiet had descended on the shop. I could hear no sound of movement, nothing.

'Are you all right, Sir?' I enquired in my best floor-walking manner. There was no reply. 'Sir?' I repeated myself.

Cautiously I approached the fitting-room and pulled back the curtain. What I saw was not a pretty sight. Our customer, if one could still describe him by that nomenclature, stood, transfixed, staring at the mirror. There was little sign of life. Just a tear trickling from the corner of each eye.

I was not surprised. He had every right to be catatonic. I thought he had taken it all rather well. I tried not to cry with him. I also tried not to laugh at him. One did not need to be Saville Row-trained to realise what had happened. There standing before me was a normally robust human being, a funny shape at the best of times, I had to admit, but nevertheless a man who had overcome his physical deformities and looked life firmly in the eye. Now he stood, all '40 SHORT PORTLY' of him, with a suit coat that fitted perfectly while the trousers hung like bermuda shorts to just 2 inches below his knee.

My tailor, Vittorio, had done it again. It takes a special kind of skill to cut 3 inches off a pair of trousers, when the instructions say lengthen 3 inches. It takes an artist to do it twice.

This was not a time for words. I undressed him as best I could, withdrew 30 pounds from the cash register and placed it in his hands, took him to the shop door, pointed him in the direction of the car park and pushed him gently, while whispering softly in his ear, 'Thank you, Sir'. He has not returned.

You would think, of course, that the only decent thing to do was blow one's brains out, or at least blow Vittorio's brains out, but being the mild-mannered person that I am, I folded the suit up, put in on the rack and concentrated the mind wonderfully on counting to one thousand.

Why I put the suit on the rack I have no idea. I just couldn't bring myself to throw it in the garbage bin. Too much of my life was wrapped up in it.

The years rolled by, the suit gathered dust, but little else. Certainly no interest . . .

One day a little rubber ball with feet, eyes, mouth, ears, bounced into my shop. 'Barry,' the mouth squeaked, 'my son's getting married and I've been all over Sydney looking for a suit and no one can fit me. What's wrong with them?'

I looked up with mild amusement. Should I tell him or not? 'Listen, me old mate, you're not going to get a bloody . . .' I stopped, frozen stiff. Could it . . . was it . . . maybe . . . what did I have to lose? ' Just one moment, Sir!' I walked over to the suit rack and pulled it out, madly dusting it down as I ushered the two of them into the fitting room. Minutes passed and I broke the world record for holding one's breath. Suddenly the silence was broken by a high-pitched scream . . . of delight! Out stepped the most satisfied customer I have every seen in my life. There he stood in an exquisite grey flannel suit that looked as if it had been tailored for him.

Unbelievable!' he said. 'I go to David Jones, Farmers, Grace Bros and half the stores in Sydney and none of those can go anywhere near fitting me, and I come to a little store near where I live and I get the perfect fit. How do you do it?'

'Well sir,' I replied in my most unctuous manner, 'we stock a special range of sizes for the discerning customer.' We were both shaking, he from disbelief, me from nervousness. 'Shall I wrap it up, Sir?' I enquired.

'My oath!' he said.

I was trying to calculate what the suit would be worth. The label had long since disappeared. The suit was of vintage quality, perfect fit. It would have cost him a fortune to have a suit tailored. My voice quavered and I looked the other way. 'Thirty-five pounds, Sir,' I croaked.

'A bloody steal!' he replied.

'Yes, Sir, that's what I was thinking!'

A SATISFIED CUSTOMER

It was one of those days when nothing much was happening. I was standing in the shop at St Ives, contemplating the meaning of life, when they walked in. Four swarthy gentlemen of southern Mediterranean appearance who, had I not known their leader personally, would have appeared sinister. 'Rocky' Fuda from the 'Fruit Bowl' was my retailing neighbour.

'Hi, what can I do for you?' I greeted him in my most cheerful retailing manner. The usually smiling Rocky and his four companions eyed me balefully.

'We wanna da suit,' they replied in unison.

'Certainly,' I replied, adjusting my demeanour to match their decidedly glum appearance. 'What size?' I enquired, reaching for my tape measure.

'Itsa no matter,' they answered.

'I beg your pardon?'

'Itsa no matter,' repeated Rocky. Had I heard correctly?

'Er ... I don't ... quite understand?' Perhaps I had better take a different tack. 'What colour did you have in mind?'

'Itsa no matter — as long as she issa dark.'

To say that I was confused is to put it lightly. 'Let me get this right. Am I to understand that you want to buy a suit and that you don't care what size it is and you don't care what colour it is, just so long as it is dark?'

'Thatsa right.'

If only every second customer could be like this, life would be very pleasant. I moved over to the suits, selected one that had been 'with us for a while', but I had to ask the obvious question. 'What if he doesn't like it? What if it doesn't fit? I'll be expected to change it for him.'

'He's notta gonna complain!' said Rocky.

'How do you know?'

'Hesa dead! Itsa for his funeral!'

IN THE GUN

Prior to the late Thursday night and Saturday afternoon shopping times, Friday afternoon was one of the busiest periods for retail stores. Travellers who arrived during that period attempting to sell their wares were given short shrift.

So when a shortish figure in a grey suit and narrow-brimmed hat, carrying two suitcases, arrived at my St Ives store one Friday afternoon, my partner, Ray Jacomb, was far from impressed.

He was barely through the door when Ray snarled, 'Not today mate.'

'But ...?'

'No buts. We don't see anyone on Friday afternoon.'

'I was told you would.'

'Well, I don't know who told you that but you were misinformed. Now hop it!'

'I've come all the way from Canberra!'

'Without an appointment? You must be crazy!'

'I thought Barry rang you.'

'Barry who?'

'Barry Cohen. Isn't this his shop?'

Barry ... Canberra ... Suddenly the penny dropped. The phone call — 'Look after Dr Gun, the Member for Kingston. He wants to buy a couple of suits ...!'

WHERE THE BUCK STOPS

DO THE RIGHT THING

One of the silliest decisions that the Federal Labor Party Parliamentary Caucus made during my time in Canberra was the introduction (after the 1975 debacle) of the midterm election for the leadership and the shadow ministry. Within hours of Gough defeating Lionel Bowen's challenge to his leadership, speculation commenced about who would challenge him when the new election was due in the middle of 1977. It was a recipe for instability.

It did not take long for many of us to realise that Gough was never going to recapture the mood of 1969 and 1972, and discussion centred around the possibility of Bill Hayden, one of the real successes of the Whitlam Ministry, challenging Gough when the opportunity presented itself.

Initially, I was one of those who encouraged Bill to run, but as the contest drew nearer I was torn between my affection and admiration for Gough and my growing conviction that Bill was our only hope of bringing us back from the massacre of 75. Few of us expected that we had much of a chance of defeating Malcolm Fraser, no matter who led the party at the next election, but many anticipated that Bill could win enough seats to put us in a good position to tackle him at the following election.

I agonised over the decision as the press and my colleagues commenced the age-old practice of counting heads. With a day to go, they had ascertained correctly that the result was nip and tuck, with only three people out of sixty-two being undecided: Ralph Jacobi, Jim McClelland and myself. It was one of the most difficult decisions I have ever had to make in politics.

With the Caucus election due on the following Tuesday, Jim McClelland invited me to join him for Thursday lunch at The Lobby restaurant, across the road from Parliament House.

The scene and the conversation are still as clear now as they were over ten years ago, as we strolled across the road on a brilliantly sunny Canberra winter's day.

'Well, son, what have you decided to do?' enquired Diamond Jim.

'Hayden!' I said.

Jim didn't hesitate with his reply. 'You're absolutely right. You've made the right decision.'

I breathed a little easier. I trusted Jim's judgement.

'You're right, Gough's had it. He's one of yesterday's men. The future lies with the Haydens and Bowens and Bill's clearly the outstanding performer in the Caucus. You've got to forget about sentiment and support the man that can get you back into Government, and Gough can't do that. Bill can!'

I knew then that I had made the right decision.

'I really am glad you've decided to support Bill,' said Jim, once again emphasising his admiration for the former Treasurer. 'But,' and there was a long pause, 'I want to tell you the reasons I am going to vote for Gough.'

I nearly tripped over my feet with shock.

'Yes,' said Jim wistfully, 'I just couldn't do it to the big bastard. After what that mongrel Kerr and Fraser did to him, I couldn't do it.'

I started to feel uncomfortable. 'I've known Gough and Margaret for over twenty-five years and frankly I couldn't look either of them in the eye again if I let them down in their hour of need.' By now I felt like a combination of Benedict Arnold and Vidkun Quisling.

'But don't you let me influence you. You stick to your guns, you're doing the right thing by the Party, the country and your own future. Don't listen to an old sentimental fool like me.'

Thanks, Jim.

The following day I flew to Sydney and then drove home

to Matcham. As I walked through the door, Rae was at the kitchen sink. As soon as she heard me come in, she spun around.

'What are you going to do?' she almost shouted at me.

'Hayden,' I replied.

Rae burst into tears. 'You bastard! How could you do it to him? After all he's been through!'

'Look, I feel the same way about him as you do, but we're talking about the future of the Australian Labor Party.'

'Bugger the Labor Party! You're talking about the greatest Prime Minister this country's ever had and you're going to give him another kick in the teeth!'

It was, as they say, a very frosty weekend, broken only by the occasional sniffle and deep, dramatic sighs.

On the following Monday night, before the ballot, I was dining once again at The Lobby, but this time with Richard Butler, Private Secretary to Gough.

'Well,' said Richard, 'have you decided?'

'Gough,' I said. 'I'll be voting for Gough!'

(Gough Whitlam defeated Bill Hayden the next day by 32 votes to 30. I have often wondered just how different our history may have been if I had stuck to my original 'firm' decision. What would Gough have done if the vote had been 31/31? The odds are almost 10/1-on that he would have resigned. Hayden would have been the Leader. There almost certainly would not have been an election until 1978. Hayden would have won seats and led us into a 1981 election, and so it goes on . . . what if only . . .?

My decision almost certainly cost me a place on Labor's front bench. I understand Hayden's supporters thought I voted for Gough, and Gough's supporters thought the opposite!)

THE MEDIUM IS THE MESSAGE

The 1977 election was in many ways as big a disaster for the Labor Party as the 1975 massacre. After two years of broken promises from Malcolm, and, one hoped, a reasonable distance away from the drama of 'the Dismissal', we expected to pick up at least the dozen or so seats traditionally held by Labor. Thanks mainly to a monumental gaffe by Gough, promising to abolish payroll tax while asking the average voter to forego a promised tax cut, the Coalition was returned with an almost identical majority. Gough resigned and this time I worked as hard as I could to get Bill Hayden elected Leader. An added thrill for me was finally making the Shadow Ministry and being appointed as Shadow Minister for Sport, Recreation, Tourism and the Environment.

I was extremely confident that if Bill could adapt himself to the requirements of the electronic media, he could give Malcolm Fraser the greatest fight of his life at the election due in 1980. However, there were changes that needed to be made. Not in substance, but in presentation.

Those who know Bill Hayden well know him to be a highly intelligent, very sensitive, hard-working human being, who, through a pretty tough childhood and experiences as a policeman, has a deep personal commitment to the Labor cause. He was an excellent Minister for Social Security, who had one of the toughest jobs imaginable in steering through the original Medicare legislation. He was also a superb Treasurer who, thanks largely to Sir John Kerr, never really got to show what he could do in that portfolio.

Those qualities, however, are not enough to get you elected to the Number One job in Australia.

Style, charisma, panache, presentation, machismo, whatever the appropriate word is to describe the magic ingredient that makes people vote for you, it was not apparent in large doses in our new Leader. Yet those who knew Bill well knew him to be a witty, interesting companion. Quite different, in fact, from the talking head he presented to the electronic media.

His speeches, while superbly written, were delivered in a flat, whining monotone that earned him the nickname of 'Willie the Whinger'. His clothes looked like early St Vincent de Paul and whenever a microphone was stuck in front of him the relaxed, friendly manner with the quick quip was replaced by a humourless, boring schoolmaster.

Bill had everything to make a great Labor Prime Minister. All he lacked was presentation. Within minutes of his elevation to the leadership, I invited him to come to my shop at St Ives to be completely outfitted from head to toe at cost price.

We decided to drive from Canberra to St Ives so the opportunity presented itself for me to give Bill a good talking to about the one ingredient he lacked. I hammered away during the four-hour drive, insisting that what he had to do was to let the real Bill Hayden be seen by the Australian people.

'You have to learn to relax in front of television and the only way to do that is to lock yourself away for a few days with some experts on TV communication and develop a more "natural style". I'm positive that if the people can get to know you as we know you, you'll kill 'em.'

I could see that Bill was resistant. He disliked intensely the idea of politics or politicians being 'packaged' like a TV product commercial. He felt that it was dishonest.

'Look, no one's asking you to change — to be anything other than yourself. The problem is that what people are seeing is not you. It's a persona you adopt whenever someone puts a mike in front of you. What I'm suggesting is that with practice you'll relax and the real you will come through, and the real you is a very attractive person. The only bit of cheating I want to do is dress you up so that people don't think they're voting for Steptoe and Son. They can accept you being hard of hearing, but not colour blind as well!'

I fingered the 30 dollar brown plaid check suit that Bill had bought with his policeman's superannuation lump sum payout. He looked at me though slitted eyes. I worked away at him throughout the rest of the trip until I was confident that I had convinced him of the changes that needed to be made.

That afternoon we spent some hours carefully outfitting him in a wardrobe that suited the image of a future Prime Minister. He looked superb and I even believed he rather fancied the new-look Bill Hayden.

That night, Rae and I, together with Bill and Dallas, joined Jim McClelland for dinner at D'Arcy's restaurant in Paddington. Warmed by wine and good food, I outlined to 'Diamond Jim' precisely what we had been discussing that day. It was one of the worst mistakes of my political career. I had barely stopped talking when the good Senator let rip.

'Bill!' he exclaimed. 'For God's sake, don't let them spoil you! You're perfect as you are now! Don't let them package you up like a bar of soap! Just be yourself!'

BEAU BILL

One of the tragedies of Australian political life is that Bill Hayden did not become Prime Minister. I'm as much to blame as anyone, but that's another story. He did, however, become an excellent Foreign Minister and Rae and I are delighted that he is to become Governor General.

In 1984, with his first official trip as Foreign Minister to the Soviet Union in the offing, he decided that he wanted to include in his itinerary a visit to the exotic region of Mongolia.

Bill's request threw his Department and the Prime

Minister's office into a tizz. Mongolia was too politically sensitive an area. Word came back from the PM's office that the trip would not be advisable. And no one was more stubborn that our erstwhile Foreign Minister, who once he got a fixation about something really dug the old proverbials in. Back went the message: 'I want to go!'. Again the PM's office advised against the idea, stating this time that it would be very difficult to organise. Bill, as is his wont, remained unmoved. 'I'm going!' he reiterated. The situation was getting desperate, John Bowan, Senior Foreign Affairs advisor to the Prime Minister, decided it would be diplomatic to see the Foreign Minister in person, in his office at Parliament House.

'Minister, we must tell you that this visit is not a good idea,' he informed Bill.

'Look,' replied Bill, jaw set firmly that told Bowan he was very determined, 'will you get this clear once and for all. I am going to Mongolia!'

There was a long pause as the PM's advisor thought pensively about what he could do to dissuade the Foreign Minister.

'I must say I cannot understand why in hell you would want to go to such a God-forsaken spot as Mongolia,' intoned Bowan. 'Unless,' he stood up and leaned across the desk to feel Bill's 1960s suit, 'you want to visit your tailor.'

GORTON SPEAK

A great bloke and a great Australian, no one could ever accuse John Gorton of being one of the great orators of the Federal Parliament. As I pointed out in my first book, *The Life of the Party*, Gough Whitlam gave 'Jolly John' a terrible time, quoting his speeches back at him and reminding him that there was 'nothing like a Liberal education'.

Here are more priceless gems from Jolly, who did more to

mangle the English language than any Prime Minister in our history.

At the Australian Botanical Gardens, October 1970: '... and if this collection here in these gardens is not thoroughly matchless and I think it probably is, but if it's not, and if it's not unique of its kind, then I have no doubt whatsoever that under the guidance of Mr Shoebridge it very shortly will be, if it isn't already.'
In a debate on the Economy on 18 February 1971, he concluded his speech thus: 'We will see in this country what we were told by the Leader of the Opposition we see abroad as a result of this Government having been in office, and that is a Government which is not subject to the gnomes of Zurich, which has strong overseas reserves, which has been enabled, through good management there, to raise Australia's good management there, to raise Australia's name high among the nations of the world and which given responsible government and opposition here, will inside this country do the same.'

A few days later on 22 February, Whitlam asked the Prime Minister a question on when he proposed to legislate for the vote for 18-year-olds: (Mr Gorton) 'I do not know on what basis the Leader of the Opposition claims, as he apparently does, that the voting of 18-, 19- and 20-year-olds in Western Australia are able to be at this stage dissected. But I can give him an undertaking that when the Government decides to present to this House matters of policy concerning this matter, he will be informed, because he will be informed shortly before they are presented to the House.'

March 1970: 'It is my understanding and it can be no more than an understanding, since it is based on my understanding, since it is based on my understanding of legal advice.'

THE THOUGHTS OF CHAIRMAN BILLY

I was travelling in India with my family and preparing a final draft of this book when I was saddened to hear of the death of Sir William McMahon, or Billy, as we all knew him. No once would ever accuse him of being one of the great Australian Prime Ministers, but from an opponent's point of view, he was always friendly and considerate. I liked the man. However he had an unerring feel for the gaffe.

I take as my text a few familiar words – that there comes a time in the life of man in the flood of time that taken at the flood leads on to fortune.
Sydney Morning Herald, 5 November 1971

Frequently when I cannot sleep at night, I have to turn to the Bible, as a means of getting six or seven hours' rest.
Bible Reading Marathon launch, 29 April 1971

McMAHON: No I didn't say that nothing was done. I said that . . . When you say that nothing was done, it depends what you mean . . .
QUESTIONER: The Government took no action?
McMAHON: That's right. The Government took no action.
Canberra, 2 October 1971

QUESTIONER: What are your thoughts on the future of Australia?
McMAHON: On what?
QUESTIONER: On the future of Australia.
McMAHON: I live here, I am proud of it. I would not want to go anywhere else and if I was anywhere else I would want to come here.
Canberra, 27 May 1971

After all, I believe in Ministerial responsibility subject of course to overall control by the Prime Minister and by Cabinet.

27 May 1971

We have to look much further and ask ourselves when we are engaged in dealings with them (the Chinese): What are we likely to gain out of it in the long term, in the medium term and in the short term as well?

Sydney, 13 May 1971

I make sure my own party is with me, even if it takes some time to persuade them.

Melbourne Herald, October 1971

The Coalition, too, is as solid as a rock.

15 March 1972

I have always been interested in Marxism as you can see from my bookshelves.

Bulletin, 10 August 1973

ONCE UPON A TIME

Playing golf with Prime Minister Bob Hawke is indeed a rare pleasure. First of all, the game has to be arranged on a first-class course on which no one else is playing on that particular day. He does not like to be kept waiting. An early morning player at Royal Canberra, where as Prime Minister he has been extended the privilege of Honorary Membership, he became particularly agitated one morning when the couple in front were slower than he thought they ought to be.

'Can't you bastards get a bloody move on?' he bellowed.

The President and Captain of Royal Canberra were not amused.

Hawke's interest in golf commenced when attending the Commonwealth Heads of Government Meeting (CHOGM) in the Bahamas. He was found under the scrutiny of TV cameras, playing with the President of Zambia, Kenneth Kaunda. Viewers in Australia saw their sporting Prime Minister bashing a Caribbean course to pieces.

Proud of his athletic prowess, he became very snarly on his return with colleagues who made unflattering remarks about his likeness to Jack Nicklaus.

Determined to eradicate this blot on his manhood, the Prime Minister set about learning the game in much the same way as he pursued the Prime Ministership. Unfortunately, he is as equally impatient and is yet to find a golf course that will surrender to his blandishments as easily as the Labor Party Caucus. He has improved considerably, however, and occasionally plays some good shots, as his recent hole-in-one will testify.

He is ably assisted by security guards who act as fore caddies. They ensure he rarely loses a ball. Playing with him at Monash some time ago, we both drove our balls into the rough on the right-hand side of a short par four 16th. Together with our partners and the security guards we searched for the two balls for the ten minutes the PM allots himself when his ball is lost, as against the fleeting glance he allocates when others suffer a similar fate.

After a few minutes, one of the security guards cried out, 'Prime Minister, are you the Golden Ram?' referring to the brand of ball I was then using. He looked wistfully towards the heavens before he eventually answered . . .'' I used to be, Comrade, I used to be!'

COHENI and JONESI

'*Yalkaparidon coheni* and *Yalkaparidon jonesi* are described here as the first-known members of the marsupial family Yalkaparidontidae and order Yalkaparidontia.' Thus began an article 'A new order of Tertiary Zalambdondont Marsupials' by Michael Archer, Suzanne Hound and Hank Godthelp in *Science* magazine of March 1988.

No one seemed surprised that two politicians, Barry Jones and me, had finally been officially declared fossils for their contribution to research being undertaken at the Riversleigh fossil find in North Queensland!

IN THE WILD

THE MENACES OF GENESIS

The following was provided for me by a land developer:

In the beginning, God created heaven and earth.

Quickly He faced legal action for failure to lodge a development application and an Environmental Impact Statement with the Council.

He was granted a temporary permit for the Heavenly part of the development, but was stymied with a Cease and Desist Order for the earthly part under the Planning Scheme Ordinance.

Appearing before the Council, God was asked why He had begun His earthly project in the first place. He replied that He just liked to be creative.

Asked how the earth was being created, God said, 'Let there be light', and immediately the council demanded to know how the light would be made. Would there be coal mining?

God explained that the light would come from a huge ball of fire.

Immediately the conservationists objected to this proposal because of the effect on the ecosystems and rainforests.

However, the timber workers also made their voices heard and they stated that the ball of fire would help the trees to grow so they could cut them down.

The members of the State Government were not prepared to comment on this project because of the forthcoming elections.

The State Government said it was a 'local' matter and not of State or Federal significance. Consequently the Council decided to take the middle path — it gave God provisional approval to make light, providing that no smoke pollution would result from this ball of fire and that He complied with the conditions of the State Pollution Control Commission and referred the ball of fire to the Board of Fire Commissioners for consent.

In addition, in order to conserve energy (and to satisfy the conservationists and timber workers) He could only have the light on half of the time.

God said that He agreed and that He would install a time switch and call the light, day and the darkness, night.

God said in reply to further questions, 'Let the earth bring forth green herb and such as may seed.'

The Council agreed, so long as native seed was used and a detailed landscape plan was submitted prior to commencement.

Having satisfied Council so far, He said, 'Let the waters bring forth the creeping creatures having life; and the fowl that may fly over the earth.'

This statement upset the Council and staff because God had not sought the permission of the National Parks and Wildlife Services, the Pastures Protection Board, the Lands Department, the Fisheries Department, the Main Roads Department, the Police Department, the Department of Aboriginal Affairs and the ACTU.

In addition, He would have to consult with the Heavenly Wildlife Federation for the Heavenly aspect of His proposal.

God was more than pleased with the 'assistance' He had received so far — He had expected a hard time, but He had been treated as a normal developer.

However, unfortunately God said He wanted to complete the project in six days!

Council officers objected strongly and said it would take God six months to prepare the Environmental Impact Statement to their satisfaction.

And God said, 'To Hell with it!'

KANGAROO

As part of a program to inform myself about the nature of the kangaroo problem I undertook a number of field trips throughout New South Wales and Queensland. The first trip was to the south-western corner of New South Wales in the Hay-Balranald district and the second to the north-western region to inspect the area around Nyngan and Warren.

Leaving Canberra by VIP plane at 4.30 in the afternoon, I was able to be out in the field with professional kangaroo shooter Chris Bryant by 6.30 pm. The purpose of this particular visit was to satisfy myself that professional shooters were killing in the most humane way possible.

Among the many absurd charges made by some extremist animal welfare groups was the allegation that professional kangaroo shooters deliberately shot kangaroos in either the spine or the stomach. As the commercial industry demands unmarked skins and untainted meat, self-interest alone demands that shooters would aim only for the head. After an hour or two with Chris, who shot ten kangaroos in a manner that caused each animal to die instantly, I was completely satisfied that the allegations were nonsense.

It was not a particularly pleasant evening but it was important for my education. As Environment Minister I had to satisfy myself about every aspect of the Kangaroo Management Plan. My job and that of my State counterparts was to ensure that various kangaroo species were maintained in substantial numbers across their broad habitat range. It was a difficult job to maintain the delicate balance between kangaroo populations and the need to ensure that Australian farmers and graziers were not overrun by roos and their livelihood endangered.

The evening's exercise over, we drove into Warren where we had arranged to have a meal at the local pub. Sergio Sergi, my cosmopolitan secretary, looked totally out of place in his black pin-striped suit, while Chris and I looked the part in our leather jackets and jeans. We were accompanied by *Age* reporter Ken Haley.

After we had finished our excellent Chinese meal, we were joined by the publican, who looked at me with signs of recognition.

'Don't I know you?' he enquired.

'Well, you may, I'm Barry Cohen, the Federal Minister for Home Affairs and the Environment.'

'I thought I recognised you from television. What the hell are you doing up here?'

'I'm up here to investigate the kangaroo situation,' I told him.

He sat down with a knowing half-smile on his face, poured himself a glass of wine and looked me straight in the eye. 'Yer wastin' yer time, mate,' he said. 'You'll never get rid of the bastards!'

ON SAFARI

There was movement at the station
    For the word had got around
    That the Minister for 'Roos was on the way . . .

The last time the hotels were booked out in Charleville was when King O'Malley rode through. With the advent of VIP planes, I was able to arrive courtesy of the big silver bird. They had come from far and wide to see this strange fellow who wanted to find out what exactly was happening regarding the kangaroo problem.

For months, farmers and graziers had been beating a path to my doorway about the enormous increase in kangaroos during the past year or two. After the drought of 1981-82, which saw a dramatic drop in the kangaroo population, mainly greys and reds and a subsequent decrease in the quota of kangaroos to be culled from three-million, to two-million, good rains had seen the population dramatically increase. Although I had permitted significant increases in the quota in 1984 and 1985, farmers were adamant that they were experiencing the biggest explosion in population for years.

'The bastards'll be eating us, if you don't increase the quota!' I was told.

Although I was cautious about any large increase, I was also conscious of the lies being spread by an unscrupulous, albeit minority, group of individuals about the state of the kangaroo population. Ill-informed conservation organisations overseas preferred to believe the liars rather than the Government. Reports coming to me from every responsible body, including the CSIRO, the universities, the State Parks and Wildlife Services, plus my own Department, indicated that the kangaroo population was on the rise, and unless something was done soon it could well get out of hand.

With my wife Rae and Environment Adviser Jonathan West, I strode down the main street of Charleville, briefcase at the ready. The Town Hall was packed as I pushed aside the swinging doors and brushed brusquely past the sullen cowboys and roo shooters leaning against the wall.

'Howdy!' I cried cheerfully, as I made my way towards the stage. I heard the dark mutterings through clenched teeth as I passed. I got the distinct impression that I was not their pin-up boy.

Next minute I was smote a mighty blow upon the arm. 'G'day!' bellowed a voice, as he grasped the one good arm I had left and shook it as if he were trying to tear it from it's socket.

'Glad you could come, mate!' the voice continued. As the mist of pain cleared from my eyes I gradually focused on the 6-foot 2-inch rawboned frame of the local Federal Member for Maranoa, Ian Cameron. 'I told yer I'd get a good mob here for yer!' he grinned. 'They've come from up to 300 hundred miles away to hear yer.' With that, Ian launched himself on to the stage and bellowed at the assembled mob.

'Righto, now listen here! The Minister's come a long way to listen to you mob and I got a list of 30 people here wanna have a yak to him. So I'll give yuz two minutes each, then sit down. Right? Okay. Shorty, you're first!'

Up the steps ambled Shorty. Black shirt, black jeans, black Stetson, black riding boots, thumbs hooked into the silver-studded belt, with spurs jingling as he walked. Out of his mouth hung a wet, limp, dead roll-your-own. Shorty's two minutes had elapsed before he made it to the mike.

'For Chrissake, get a bloody move on, Shorty. We haven't got all day!' The lean, leathery figure was unmoved by his local Member's urging. He droned on for a few minutes before he was told, 'That's it mate, you've had yer two minutes. Now piss off!'

I sat there on the stage, mesmerised by this banter between elected representative and constituent. Those that followed were given the same treatment. 'Sit down, shut up, piss off, get a bloody move on', were the elegant phrases that tumbled from the lips of the sunburned Member for Maranoa. My surprise at the way he addressed the 'voters' was only matched by sheer amazement at the way in which it was accepted. They were neither amazed nor amused. They were quite impassive. I realised I had left the big city a long way behind.

The consultation went on all afternoon as I listened to the views of the country folk. The professional kangaroo shooters urging increased culling quotas may well have been talking through their pockets, but there were no financial incentives for the graziers to advocate a reduction in numbers, except to protect their properties. One could not but be impressed by the sincerity with which they argued their case.

If I thought I had left the big smoke far behind during that first day in Southern Queensland, it was nothing to the next day's experience. While I had pointed out in my first book that I had overcome my 'Fear of Flying', I still caste a wary eye over every aircraft in which I was travelling. So it was that I approached the journey to Charleville Airport with a slight case of apprehension, having been informed by my genial host, the mild-mannered Member for Maranoa, that Rae and I were to accompany him in a small plane to inspect the property of one 'Mac' Patterson.

'Mac', I was informed, would do the honours by piloting us in his own plane.

As we waited on the tarmac for the Learjet to arrive, I heard in the heavens the coughing, spluttering and farting of an aeroplane clearly distressed. My fears for the pilot were obvious.

'The poor bastard!' I cried.

'That's Mac!' shouted Ian, as he set off down the runway to await the arrival of his good friend. I watched in horror as a dyspeptic matchbox bumped and ground its way down the tarmac to the excited whoops of the Local Member. When it finally lurched to a grinding halt, out jumped the moleskinned, riding-booted figure of 'Mac' Patterson.

'G'DAY, PLEASED TO MEETCHA!' he roared, as he squeezed the hand that had only just started to recover from yesterday's bruising. Once again, tears came to my eyes as I struggled to unleash myself from the vice-like grip. 'SORRY I CAN'T SHAKE HANDS WITH MY RIGHT HAND!' he roared again, as he waved his other hand encased in plaster. 'HAD A BIT OF A FIGHT WITH A BULL YESTERDAY AND THE BULL WON!' he laughed, or rather screamed. By now, my ears were hurting almost as much as my hand. So far, 'Mac' had not spoken a word below ninety decibels.

'Mac's a bit hard of hearing,' Ian whispered in my ear.

'So will I be if he doesn't shut up,' I whispered back. By now he had released my hand and the blood was starting to circulate again. As the numbness gradually wore off, my mind focused on the Wright Bros creation sitting beside us on the tarmac.

'You're not suggesting we actually fly in that thing?' I enquired in my best Ministerial manner.

'BEEN DOWN FOUR TIMES, NEVER BEEN SERIOUSLY BENT!' he shouted. The thought occurred to me that it was a shame the bull hadn't gone for his throat.

'Mac,' I said, 'you don't have to speak quite so loud. I'm in Charleville, not Canberra.'

'SORRY MATE, BIT HARD OF HEARING!' he bellowed, coming down to about eighty decibels.

'You'll excuse me if I ask what may seem a rather foolish question, old chap, but exactly how do you manage to fly that thing with only one hand?'

'BIT TRICKY!' he roared again, 'BUT SHE'LL BE RIGHT!' echoing the confidence of the Australian bushman down through the years.

I was still far from convinced by the contraption 'Mac' was urging Rae, Ian and me to board. He noticed my furrowed brow.

'NO WORRIES! IF SHE LOOKS LIKE GOING DOWN I'LL JUST LINE HER UP WITH A COUPLA TREES AND KNOCK THE WINGS OFF TO GET RID OF THE FUEL TANKS. THAT'LL STOP HER BURSTING INTO FLAMES' he told me, reassuringly.

'Oh, well, that's all right,' said I relieved. I thought for a moment there was something to worry about.' What sort of maniac was I being let loose with? My mind turned to fantasising about suitable tortures for Cameron. But coward that I am, I am even more afraid of letting people know I'm a coward. Cravenly I crept abroad, closed my eyes and prayed to the One True God, Jehovah. What, I thought, in His name, am I doing here? Why did Hawke hate me so much? Why hadn't he given me something like Veterans' Affairs, or Education, or Health, or anything that kept me in nice, safe, warm places like RSL clubs, or schools or hospices for the dying? 'Why,' I cried, 'am I always risking my neck inspecting the bloody environment?'

It was too late now. We were airborne. I tried to gather my shattered nerves and listen to 'Mac's' description of the problems of the man on the land.

I can't recall how far it was to 'Mac's' property 'Wellclose' but I do know that it was a modest thousand square miles in size. We chugged and coughed and spluttered along for almost an hour before 'Mac' announced, 'THERE SHE IS.' He banked the plane steeply and started pointing excitedly at spots of interest. 'THERE'S THE HOUSE . . . THE DAM . . .' I wasn't listening. I had noticed that, as he banked the plane, he was pointing with his one good hand. I tapped him on the shoulder.

'Mac,' I said, seriously. 'I don't wish to interfere, but would it be too much to ask you to use at least one of your hands to fly the plane?'

'OH! SORRY MINISTER I WAS GETTING CARRIED AWAY!' He grinned, grabbed the stick and taxied into land. Just as I thought the worst of it was over, 'Mac' gave a shriek. 'ROOS!' he screamed. 'ROOS!!' and the plane took off. Not into the air, but into the bushes. 'Mac' had spotted a group of greys grazing peacefully among the trees on the left of what passed laughingly for an airfield. Next minute our pilot was whooping like a young boy as we zig-zagged through the gum trees at full throttle, chasing the kangaroos. 'SEE, I TOLD YOU THEY WERE EVERYWHERE!'

'Yes . . . Yes . . . I think you've made your point!' I gasped as we taxied back to the 'airfield', before finally we were driven to the homestead.

Rae, Ian and I were to spend the rest of the afternoon with the delightful Patterson family. An intelligent, well-read man, 'Mac' was the quintessential Australian farmer. A man who lived on and loved the land and all the creatures on it. I was to see literally thousands of kangaroos in one afternoon. All 'Mac' was asking for was a balance between kangaroos and his livelihood.

THE ULURU EXPRESS

Uluru National Park, better known as Ayers Rock and the Olgas, undertook a remarkable transformation during the latter years of the Fraser Government and the early years of the Hawke Government. With the magnificent Yulara Village, a new jet airport, the clean-up of grotty old motels and new interpretive work, the Park had become, by the time I ceased to be Minister for Arts, Heritage and Environment, the equal of anything in the world.

While I would be delighted to have history record that it was all due to my efforts, it was due in no small way to the determined and dedicated efforts of one of the best public servants I know: the Director of the Australian National Parks and Wildlife Service, Professor Derrick Ovington. A small, quietly spoken, almost shy person, Derrick had only two minor flaws. Despite spending a major portion of his life in the Great South Land, he still retained a North of England accent that I found totally incomprehensible. He also had a streak of stubbornness that made a mule look positively wimpish.

Our success in upgrading the Park was marred by our being unable to convince the geniuses in the Department of Finance that they should part with the three or four million dollars necessary to build a decent bitumen road from Ayers Rock to the Olgas, to match the excellent road already built from Yulara Village and the airport to the Rock itself. Each year the track through fragile sandy red desert got deeper and deteriorated further, as the number of tourist buses and cars doubled and trebled, along with the dramatic increase in tourism. Each year the money needed to build the road exceeded the CPI figures.

During the Spring of 1986 at about the time that Laurie Brereton was running into flak over his Darling Harbour Monorail proposal, I undertook a tour of Kakadu and Uluru to inspect the work that had been done during the past year or two. On the flight from Darwin to Ayres Rock I fantasised about the reaction from the Greenies if I were to announce that we would build a monorail from the Rock to the Olgas. I was almost tempted to announce it just for the fun of seeing their reaction. At that moment the good Professor hove into view.

'Derrick, I've got a great idea to solve your road problem to the Olgas,' I said with a deadly serious expression on my face.

'So have I, Barry!'

'What's yours?'

'A monorail!'

My joke had fallen flat. 'That's what I was going to say', I said with a big grin.

'Well, you're right. It's a wonderful idea.' The grin froze as I listened in mounting horror as my Director outlined in detail his proposal. On a number of occasions I tried to interrupt him, but the dear fellow ploughed on regardless as figures, statistics, technical data and what have you spewed forth. Finally I could stand it no longer.

'Derrick,' I said finally, 'I was joking.'

Undeterred he continued.

'Derrick,' I found myself shouting, 'I was bloody joking. We'd be the laughing stock of the nation. It's the maddest idea I have heard. Technically it may work, but environmentally and aesthetically it would be a disaster! The Greenies would go ape and they would have my total support.'

For the first time I think it dawned on him that I was serious but during the next few days, he never missed the opportunity to raise the matter again and again. Finally, on our last day as we stood at the foot of the Olgas, looking back towards the Rock, I heard the dulcet tones of the good Professor intone . . . 'The monorail would go along . . .' I could stand it no longer.

'DERRICK, THAT F...ING MONORAIL WILL BE BUILT OVER MY DEAD BODY! DO YOU UNDERSTAND?'

It was never mentioned again. I had finally killed the idea ... I thought.

Almost a year to the day, no longer a Minister, I was being driven to Parliament House when I opened the *Daily Telegraph* –.

'Minister for Arts, Sport, Tourism, Recreation, Heritage, etc. etc., Mr John Brown, today announced that a MONORAIL would be built from Ayres Rock to ...'

The Commonwealth driver almost drove off the road as I hissed, 'DERRICK!!'

AIRPORT 74

Before I entered Parliament in 1969, one of the major issues was the site of Sydney's second international airport. Everyone wants airports, but not in their area. The result was that no matter what site was selected, the opposition was instant and vociferous. There were almost as many suggested locations as there were planes, and protest groups were formed as soon as a new location was mentioned. Towra Point, Richmond, Somersby, Galston and Badgery's Creek were among the numerous places that were fancied and were the subject of violent debate and abuse of the Government of the day.

The Whitlam Government's handling of the issue was not one of its finest performances. The one site that the Government could not afford to support, as had each of its successors, was the most cost effective but politically disastrous suggestion that the problem be solved by having dual runways at the existing airport at Kingsford Smith. Four seats, all held by Labor, were nearby. Galston, on the North Shore, was thought to be the most politically acceptable site for the second airport. The result was a big swing against the Whitlam Government in the Parramatta by-election in September 1973.

Suddenly the idea surfaced that Badgery's Creek, in the south-western part of Sydney, would be an ideal site. At the time Tom Uren was Minister for Urban and Regional Development. Although not the Minister for Environment, Tom prided himself on being the most environmentally conscious Minister in the Whitlam Government.

When he came out in support of the second airport being located at Badgery's Creek, Dr Dick Klugman, the Member for Prospect, in whose electorate the airport was to be located and an arch enemy of the conservation movement, sent a very curt telegram to his parliamentary colleague:

DEAR MINISTER

AM DEEPLY SHOCKED AT YOUR SUPPORT FOR BADGERY'S CREEK AS THE SITE FOR SYDNEY'S SECOND INTERNATIONAL AIRPORT. AREN'T YOU AWARE THAT THE PROPOSED SITE IS ON SOME OF THE OLDEST LAND IN AUSTRALIA.

THE IMPOSTER

Dr Dick Klugman, Labor Member for Prospect since 1969 and an expert at getting up the noses of conservationists, had the following telegram exchange with a Labor colleague during the latter part of 1985.

DR R. E. KLUGMAN
PARLIAMENT HOUSE
CANBERRA :ACT

DEAR COLLEAGUE
STRONGLY RECOMMEND YOU SUPPORT MINISTER COHEN IN HIS STAND TO PROTECT TASMANIAN WILDERNESS. I BELIEVE HIS ADVICE

IS BALANCED AND REASONABLE AND WILL PROTECT JOBS AND THE ENVIRONMENT. IT IS ESSENTIAL THE FEDERAL ALP STRENGTHEN ITS PRO-ENVIRONMENT IMAGE AND BUILDS SUPPORT TO THE PRO-ENVIRONMENT PUBLIC.

BOB CARR MP
NEW MINISTER FOR PLANNING AND ENVIRONMENT

He sent the following telegram in reply:

HON. BOB CARR, MP
PARLIAMENT HOUSE
MACQUARIE STREET
SYDNEY

DEAR BOB,
SHOULD WARN YOU SOMEBODY PRETENDING TO BE YOU HAS SENT ME SILLY TELEGRAM STOP HAVE NOTIFIED FEDERAL POLICE.

DICK KLUGMAN

THE SWAMP FOX

Peter Doyle, Sydney's best-known fish restaurateur, was in his youth a fisheries inspector. Young and eager, he approached his first appointment at a New South Wales coastal town with enthusiasm and zeal. Shortly after his arrival he become aware of the nefarious activities of the district's most notorious poacher of fish, one 'Paddles' Newton.

The Ned Kelly of the underwater world, Paddles had pitted his wits against the Department of Fisheries 'finest' and won. Despite their best attempts to land him, he had avoided with consummate ease every trap set by Peter's predecessor. Doyle was warned by the locals not to run the risk of embarrassment by trying to catch the resourceful and slippery Paddles.

The more he heard of his reputation as an 'uncatchable' the more our fearless inspector determined he would succeed where others before him had failed. For weeks he scoured the foreshores and the mangrove swamps, searching for the telltale signs of the traps. Just when he was on the verge of acknowledging Paddles' supremacy and giving up the chase, he came across some of the most skilfully laid traps he had ever seen, set carefully in the mangrove swamps. This, surely, was the work of a master craftsman.

Determined to catch Paddles red-handed, he lashed himself to the mangrove trees and awaited the visit of the villain himself. As the hours ticked by and the chill factor rose, young Peter Doyle wondered at the wisdom of his action. Tired and shivering, half-chewed by mosquitoes, he was on the verge of giving up the chase when, as the early morning mist started to rise off the swamps, he spied the shadowy figure of Paddles, creeping tippy-toed through the mangroves.

Doyle stiffened, flattened himself against the tree, held his breath and tried desperately to blend into the environment.

The bearded and ragged figure of the old swamp fox glided stealthily nearer until eventually he was only feet away from both Doyle and the first of the traps.

After nervous, darting looks left and right, Paddles dropped down and hauled the trap up out of the water. In a flash our intrepid young inspector leapt forward and placed his arm on Paddles' shoulders. 'Gotcha, Paddles!' shouted the triumphant officer.

Paddles swung round as if he had been shocked by an electric eel. 'Jesus Christ!' he exclaimed. 'Who are you?'

'DOYLE, FISHERIES INSPECTOR!!'

Paddles didn't bat an eyelid. 'Thank Christ for that! For a moment I thought you owned the bloody traps!'

SAVING THE REEF

It was the first meeting of the Great Barrier Reef Marine Park Ministerial Council to be held at the same time as the opening of the Great Barrier Reef Wonderland in Townsville.

Sir Joh was there, representing Queensland, while John Brown and I represented the Federal Government. Also present were the Chairman of the Authority, Graeme Kelleher, and its other two members, Dr Joe Baker, head of the Australian Institute of Marine Science, and Sir Sydney Schubert, Queensland Co-ordinator General. This was the final decision-making body on matters concerning Australia's greatest natural treasure.

For years the Queensland and Federal Governments had been criticised by academics and conservationists for not doing enough to save the reef from damage by the crown of thorns starfish. Shortly after I became Minister, I managed to convince Cabinet to provide three-quarters of a million dollars for research. The problem was that Queensland was quite happy for us to go it alone. The Chairman of the Authority, one of the most talented public servants I have ever met, went to great pains to explain to Joh the need for Queensland to make a contribution.

'It's very serious, Mr Premier,' explained the gentle Kelleher. 'Up to 35 per cent of the Reef has been damaged by the crown of thorns starfish.'

Sir Joh would have none of that. 'Now, Graeme, you've only been on this . . . this Reef . . . for eight . . . eight years. I've been . . . on the reef . . . a long time . . . ten . . . twenty . . . my goodness, yes . . . twenty years. Twenty years ago . . . Robert . . . Dr . . . Endean, took me out to show me . . . Reef . . . Great Barrier Reef . . . twenty years ago . . . Yes, my word . . . and there, they showed me the damage done just two weeks before by a plague of starfish. And I looked at the Reef . . . the starfish and after two weeks . . . only two weeks ... my goodness yes ... it was all glistening white and healthy. So you don't ... you don't ... have to tell me ... no, about the crown of starfish ... thorns. I've been here longer ... longer than you ... yes, my word I have!'

A strange silence settled over the meeting. Hardened public servants shuffled papers nervously, looking at their feet, the ceiling, anywhere but at Australia's next nomination for the Nobel Prize. Finally, Graeme broke the silence.

'Mr Premier,' he answered softly. 'The only reason that it is white is that it is DEAD!'

SLEIGHT OF HAND

If Graeme Kelleher, Chairman of the Great Barrier Reef Marine Park Authority, does nothing else, the nation will forever be indebted to him for the establishment of the Great Barrier Reef Wonderland. With extraordinary diplomacy and skill he managed to convince the Queensland and Federal Governments, together with the private sector, to put some twenty million dollars into a magnificent complex on the water's edge at Townsville, which includes a major display by the Queensland Museum, an Omnimax Theatre, a range of quality shops and boutiques, alongside an excellent reef interpretive centre. The centrepiece is an aquarium containing one of the few living coral reefs on land.

I was fascinated to hear our Prime Minister claim the credit for it, when he jointly opened it with Sir Joh during the 1987 election campaign. My mind went back to the Budget Cabinet discussions when Graeme and I had pleaded for a modest twenty-one staff to run the Federal Government's section of Wonderland. Since 1983, the Government had been trying to reduce the number of public servants, and each year Ministers fought against Treasury and Finance to prevent further staff cuts. I accepted that new technology should allow reasonable reductions, but not when the Cabinet was making decisions to vastly increase the workload and activities of the Department. The problem was that from one Budget to another like was not being compared with like. Having set up or expanded a whole range of new institutions (museums, national parks, rainforest projects, etc.,) I was livid when Finance Minister Peter Walsh and Treasurer Paul Keating, kept telling me my Department had one of the biggest percentage increases in staff and funds of any portfolio. 'Maybe I have,' I replied, 'but I've also had the biggest increase in the jobs I have to do.'

When the Great Barrier Reef Wonderland came up for discussion during the 1987 Budget talks, Cabinet, and Hawke in particular, went off their collective face when I asked for twenty-one extra staff.

'We've promised the nation we'd cut staff levels!' they cried.

'Well, what do you think I'm going to run the place with — Boy Scouts? Twenty's the bare minimum!'

Hawke moaned and groaned and rolled his eyes. No decision was made. Over the next couple of months the matter came before Cabinet three times. Finally, in exasperation, I said 'Look, if it's the staff levels only you're worried about, I can accept twelve on staff and employ eight on contract. That way they won't show up on the ASL [Average Staff Levels]. Of course it'll cost you $20,000 more!'

Hawke beamed. Sir Humphrey would have been proud of him.

Senator Malcolm Scott (Liberal WA)
Let me say the only reason why Tasmania has to rely on sea transport is that it is an island off the mainland of Australia.

THE LAST DUMP

If anyone wants to dump foreign material in Commonwealth waters under the *Sea Dumping Act*, they are required to apply for permission to the Federal Minister for the Environment. During my four and a half years in that position, I signed many permits involving various companies, individuals, State and local governments to dump material in Commonwealth waters. Most of the requests were fairly predictable and unexceptional. I was, however, a little taken aback when an officer of my Department arrived hot and flustered at my office requesting my signature in a hurry.

'What's the rush?' I asked.
'It's got to be signed today!'
'What the hell for?'
'Well, it's a rather delicate matter.'
'Delicate?' I snorted. 'Delicate? Since when is dumping rubbish at sea a matter of delicacy?'
'Well this is. You see, it's a body!'
'A body of what?'
'A human body! The funeral's tomorrow.'

Senator Tom Drake-Brockman — April 1970
We could have pilots undergo a crash course of three months.

INDEX OF NAMES

ACHESON, Lady Caroline 30
ACHESON, Lady Isabella 30
ACHESON, Viscount 29–30
ALI, Mohammed 17
ARCHER, Bernard 78
ARCHER, Dr Michael 159
ARMITAGE, John 65
ARNOLD, Benedict 149

BAKER-FINCH, Ian 16
BAKER, Dr Joe 177
BANANA, Dr Joseph 82–3
BANANA, Mrs 83
BATES, Mr 121
BATHEY, A.B. 102
BERT, 86–90
BISHOP, Reg 50–1
BJELKE-PETERSEN, Sir Joh 177–8
BLEWETT, Dr Neal 68
BOWAN, John 154
BOWEN, Lionel 18, 48–9, 148–9
BRERETON, Laurie 58–9, 169
BROWN, John 15–17, 72, 171
BRYANT, Chris 164
BUGNER, Joe 16–17
BUGNER, Marlene 16–17
BURLEY GRIFFIN, Walter 112
BURY, Brian 38
BUSSELL, Fred 109
BUTLER, Richard 150
BUTTON, John 36–8

CAIRNS, Dr Jim 76

CAMERON, Ian 166–70
CAPEWELL, Phil 125
CARR, Bob 174–5
CARRIER, Robert 136
CAVANAGH, Jim 50
CHALFONT, Lord 47
CHANEY Snr, Fred 6–7
CHAPPELL, Greg 16
CHARLES, Prince 41–2
CHIFLEY, Ben 64, 100, 101
CHILCOTT, Monica 123
CHIPP, Don 35–6
CLOUGH, Mr 99
COHEN, Adam 80, 122
COHEN, Angelique 128
COHEN, Aree 128
COHEN, Barry 2–5, 10–12, 13–14, 15, 16, 17, 18, 19, 20–22, 24, 28–31, 32–6, 39–40, 41, 44–5, 51–2, 53, 58–60, 63, 65, 66–9, 72–4, 77, 79–81, 82–3, 86–8, 94–9, 102–10, 111–13, 116–37, 139–45, 148–54, 158, 159, 162, 164–5, 166–70, 171–3, 174.
COHEN, Donna Lee 128
COHEN, Julai 128, 130–31
COHEN, Jules 72
COHEN, Martin 120–2
COHEN, Louis 79
COHEN, Paul 128–31
COHEN, Rae 11–12, 15, 16–17, 41, 77, 79–81, 83, 102–5, 116–37, 149–50, 166–70.

COHEN, Suzi 72
COHEN, Stuart 122, 125
COHEN, Suzie 72
COLBOURNE, Bill 94
CONNOLLY, David 52-3
CONWAY, Peter 14
COOMBE, David 110
CURTIN, John 64, 100

DALY, Fred 50, 60, 99-100
DANGAR, Mrs 33-6
DE SADE, Marquis 22
DIANA, Princess 41-2
DOUGLAS, Kirk 78
DOYLE, Peter 175-6
DOYLE, Tony 40
DRUMMOND, Peter 106
DUCKER, John 97
DUFFY, Alanna 22
DUFFY, Caroline 22
DUFFY, Michael 3, 20-2, 23
DUNN, Hugh 127

EDDINGTON, Hugo 77
EDDINGTON, Paul 77
EDDINGTON, Tricia 77
ELGIN, Lord 52
ENDEAN, Dr Robert 177
EVANS, D.S. 19
EVANS, Gareth 3-5

FERRER, Jose 131-2
FLOWERS, Ann 60-1
FOREST, Lord 106
FOWLER, Kath 132
FOWLER, Terry 132
FRASER, Malcolm 12, 66, 110, 148-9, 151, 171
FREE, Ross V. 72
FREUDENBERG, Graham 53-4
FRY, Bob 13-14
FUDA, Rocky 143-4

GAIR, Vince 35
GALVIN, Pat 9-10, 16-17
GEITZELT, Arthur 111
GEORGE 103-5
GERALDINE 77

GODTHELP, Hank 159
GOSFORD, Lord 28-9
GOSFORD, Lady Lynette 31
GORTON, Sir John 6, 154-5
GRIFFITHS, Alan 112
GRATTAN, Michelle 4
GROVES, Joy 40
GUN, Dr. Ritchie 144-5

HALEY, Ken 165
HARTLEY, Bill 110
HAWKE, Bob 3, 16, 53-4, 73, 82, 111, 157-8, 169, 171, 178-9
HAWTHORN, Nigel 78
HAYDEN, Bill 47, 50, 82, 106, 148-54
HAYDEN, Dallas 153
HEALY, Agnes 98
HEALY, Jack 98
HILL, Gordon 106, 108
HILL, Robert 81
HODGMAN, Michael 65-6
HOLDING, Clyde 4-5
HOUND, Suzanne 159
HOLLIS, Colin 68
HOWARD, John 52
HUGGETT, Libby 123
HUMPHREYS, Ben 21, 72
HURFORD, Chris 111

JACOBI, Ralph 148
JACOMB, Ray 144-5
JAMES, Bert 64-5
JAMES, Clive 14
JAMES, Rowley 64
JONES, Barry 72, 73-4, 158-9
JONES, Charlie 47-8

KAUNDA, Kenneth 82, 158
KEATING, Paul 101, 179
KELLEHER, Graeme 177-8, 179
KELLY, Ned 175
KELLY, Ros 5, 22, 72
KENDALL, Henry 59-60
KENNEDY, Graham 14
KENNELLY, Pat 100
KERR, Alan 17
KERR, Sir John 149, 151

KHAN, Genghis 34
KILLEN, Sir James 63, 65–6
KINSLEY, Michael 57
KIRWAN, Frank 106
KLUGMAN, Dick 174, 175
KUNTZ, Dr. 49–50

LANDA, Paul 40
LANG, Jack 100–1
LETTE, Kathy 60
LILLEE, Dennis 16
LINSKY, Susie 132
LINSKY, Tom 132
LUSHER, Cherie 83
LUSHER, Stephen 82

MANDERSON, Dr. Lenore 10
MAO, Chairman 74
MARTIN, Lionel 132–3
MARX, Groucho 122
MAY, Ricky 16
MACKAY, Dr. Malcolm 63
McCLELLAND, Doug 102
McCLELLAND, Freda 102–5
McCLELLAND, Jim 8–9, 58, 102–5, 148–9, 153
McCLELLAND, Lorna 1, 102
McHUGH, Jeanette 68, 83
McLEAY, Janet 82
McLEAY, Leo 82, 95
McMAHON, John 95
McMAHON, Sir William 24, 156–7
McMICHAEL, Dr. Don 9
McNICHOLL, David 48–51
MENADUE, John 50
MENGITSU, President 82
MILDREN, John 14–15, 23
MILLIGAN, Spike 136–7
MILNE, Greg 28
MOI, President 82
MOLLISON, James 24–5
MOORE, John 82
MORRISON, Bill 50
MUGABE, Robert 82
MURPHY, Ingrid 119
MURPHY, Lionel 119–20
MURRAY, Jan 15–16, 17

NEWTON, Paddles 175–6
NEWTON, Jack 16
NICKLAUS, Jack 158
NORMAN, Greg 18

O'MALLEY, King 165
ORMONDE, Jim 102
OVINGTON, Prof. Derrick 171–3

PACKER, Sir Frank, 48, 78–9
PATTERSON, Mac 168–70
PEACOCK, Andrew 52
PEARSALL, The Family 128
PICKERING, Larry 65

QUISLING, Vidkun 149

RAY, Robert 72
REID, Gordon 67
RICHARDSON, Graham 17, 21, 24–5, 112–13
ROBERTSON, Agnes 60
ROBERTSON, Clive 61
ROBERTSON, Sir John 59–60

SANSOM, Tony 11, 41
SANTAMARIA, Bob 76, 98
SAW, Andrew 135–6
SCHOLES, Gordon 9
SCHUBERT, Sir Sydney 177
SCOTT, Malcolm 6–7
SCULLIN, Jim 100
SERGI, Leigh 15–16
SERGI, Sergio 11, 15, 72–3, 86–91, 164
SHOEBRIDGE, Mr. 155
SHORTY, 167
SIBRAA, Kerry 81
SIBRAA, Yvonne 83
SIM, Peter 6–7
SIMONS, Lyn 67
SIMPSON, Gary 135–6
SIMPSON, Joan 135–6
SNEDDEN, Sir Billy 32
SWADLING, Dennis 40

TERNEN, Kerry 125
THATCHER, Margaret 35

THELMA, 67–8
TINGLE, John 45
TOBY, Clive 32–3
TRAVERS, Mary 131

UNSWORTH, Barry 28, 41, 58
UREN, Tom 174

VIDAL, Gore 135
VITTORIO 142

WALSH, Peter 3, 179
WARD, Eddie 64
WARNOCK, Mary 61
WEDGEWOOD-BENN, Anthony 30
WEST, Johnathan 166
WEST, Stewart 3
WHEELDON, John 5–6, 8–9, 75, 76, 135–6
WHEELDON, Judy 134–6
WHITLAM, Gough 35, 36, 44–53, 63, 110–11, 119, 148–50, 151, 154–5, 172
WHITLAM, Margaret 120, 149
WILDE, Oscar 135
WILLIAMS, R. M. 19
WRAN, Neville 28, 53–5, 58

YOUNG, Sir Harold 81
YOUNG, Mick 111

FOR THE BEST IN PAPERBACKS, LOOK FOR THE
PENGUIN

Rockchoppers: Growing Up Catholic in Australia   Edmund Campion

Nicknames such as micks, paddies and rockchoppers showed that for decades Catholics were second best in Australia.

In Rockchoppers, Edmund Campion looks at the influences on this tribal group of Australians. Outside the church an unfriendly society seemed to menace them. In response, they turned from the loyalties of a Protestant dominated society and created their own defensive structures, such as the Movement of B. A. Santamaria.

In exploring the experience of contemporary Catholics in a colonial culture, Edmund Campion provides insights into the wider issues of a religious minority finding its place in a pluralist society.

'A major contribution to our cultural history.'
John McLaren, *Australian Book Review*

'Campion's lively and in many ways controversial account is both a personal history of growing up Catholic and an historian's view of how the institution itself has grown . . .'
D. J. O'Hearn, *Australian Society*

'Anyone who wants to understand Australian society and politics should read it.'   Richard Hall, *National Times*

FOR THE BEST IN PAPERBACKS, LOOK FOR THE

PENGUIN

Shouting from China Helene Chung

Shouting from China records the triumphs and frustrations of the ABC's first woman foreign correspondent in Beijing. Helene Chung reveals China's ambivalent attitude to overseas Chinese and the continuing link between Chinese villagers and their relatives in Australia. She examines the dilemma of seeking to modernize using western technology without western ideas. Although economic reform has led to unparalleled prosperity in China, it has increased the opportunity for crime, polarized rich and poor and posed a threat to the one-Party state.

In describing the problems radio journalists face trying to be heard shouting from China over inadequate telephone lines and poor connections, trying to report from a closed communist country, from a position of segregation and cultural isolation, Helene Chung has created an absorbing picture of daily life in China, and has presented it with the particular insight of an overseas Chinese, so called even though she is a fourth-generation Tasmanian.

FOR THE BEST IN PAPERBACKS, LOOK FOR THE

PENGUIN

Around the Bend   John Hepworth and John Hindle
Illustrated by Geoff Prior

In an improbable adventure, three middle-aged eccentrics challenged the wild (and the tame) on an epic raft voyage down the mighty Murray River, from the mountains to the sea. 'Forty-nine days ... we might have gone faster, but we kept meeting people ...'

What the Dickens!   Barry Dickens

Barry Dickens' writing has established him as the rather zany, eccentric voice of the wag in the pub. His true Australian wit comes through in this hilarious stumble through everyday Australia.

Adam and Eve and Armageddon   John Shakespeare

A cartoon book taking a humorous look at the bible and Christianity. The cartoons are based on well-known bible stories and use familiar figures such as Noah, Eve and Samson to satirize various aspects of fundamentalist Christianity as well as those quirks of human nature which are as common now as they have ever been.

The Penguin Leunig
Michael Leunig

'Leunig's subjects are as ambitious as his technique is simple. World cataclysm, The Flood, loneliness, cruelty, lust and greed ... Sometimes whimsical, this prodigiously gifted artist is never guilty of Whimsey, and, mercifully, he is never 'relevant', 'socially aware' or 'narrowly political'.

FOR THE BEST IN PAPERBACKS, LOOK FOR THE 🐧

PENGUIN

Four books by KERRY CUE

Hang On To Your Horses Doovers

In this hilarious guide to eating out and eating in Kerry Cue addresses such issues as: The Rise and Fall of the Tuna Casserole, Everyday Etiquette for Couth Australians and Eating Out for Pleasure and Sexual Gain.

Born to Whinge

From filling the baby's inner ear with mashed pumpkin to converting the family car to a four-wheeled Gladbag *Born to Whinge* is a hilarious celebration of the bizarre job of being a parent. It is the funniest and most thoroughly unreliable guide to parenting on the market today.

Crooks, Chooks and Bloody Ratbags

Crooks, Chooks and Bloody Ratbags is a hilarious tale of life in a small country town and its police station – cops and crooks, locals and landed gentry, and in the middle of it all the Meehan family.

Another Bloody Ratbag Book

Another Bloody Ratbag Book is a highly enjoyable continuation of the Meehan mayhem encountered for the first time in *Crooks, Chooks, and Bloody Ratbags*.

FOR THE BEST IN PAPERBACKS, LOOK FOR THE

PENGUIN

The Roo Book Neil Curtis

This rooful country has been rooted in bush legend too long. Neil Curtis takes the inscrootable roo and liberates it. Roos run riot in his hilarious drawings, satirizing Australians and poking fun at nearly everything.

A Bunyip Close Behind Me Eugénie McNeil and Eugénie Crawford

Eugénie McNeil's delightfully witty recollections of Sydney in the 1890s have been retold by her daughter Eugénie Crawford. Historian, Humphrey McQueen has written of this book: 'perfect in its own way ... at once witty, informative, vivacious and wise.'

Two books by NANCY KEESING
Illustrated by Victoria Roberts

Lily on the Dustbin

Australian families can 'talk till the cows come home'. Nancy Keesing has collected examples of hilarious and down-to-earth expressions of women and their families from all over Australia.

Just Look Out the Window

In her new book, the prolific and inquisitive editor of *Shalom* and *Lily on the Dustbin* has collected a wide range of superstitions current in the Australian community. Every aspect of our multicultural community is represented, and illustrations are by the whimsical and amusing cartoonist Victoria Roberts.